CW01676576

ME, MY FAMILY AND THE POLTERGEIST

ME, MY FAMILY AND THE POLTERGEIST
BOOK ONE

DIANA TOWNSEND

USSONS

INTRODUCTION

My daughter Lucy was visiting with her partner when she asked the question.

"Mum, can you tell Dave about the White Lady?"

I looked up in surprise.

"Why me? You were the one who spoke to her."

"Mum!" Lucy said indignantly. "I was four when we left Silverlands. I hardly remember anything about it."

"Seriously?"

I felt a strange mixture of surprise and sadness. Silly, really. I should have realised that, to a young woman, something that happened twenty years ago might as well have taken place in the Middle Ages. To her, it was a lifetime ago, but to me, those days still seemed as clear as yesterday.

And if Lucy had forgotten, perhaps Claire and Michael had forgotten too.

It was then that I decided to write an account of what had occurred as a permanent record for my daughters, Claire and Lucy, and for my nephew, Michael.

After all, it is not every family that gets to share their home with a poltergeist.

CHAPTER 1

As a teenager, I didn't believe in ghosts.

I loved reading ghost stories, of course, and watching horror films, but if anyone had tried to tell me that ghosts, ghouls and things-that-go-bump-in-the-night really existed, I would have laughed at them.

Everyone knew ghosts were nothing more than superstitious nonsense, didn't they?

Back then, it had all seemed so simple.

But first, I had better explain about myself and my family.

As a child, I always knew that my parents were different. Not different in a bad way, but different. A little eccentric, perhaps. A little bit more creative than most. It didn't bother me, though, because I loved them and I was proud of them.

Mum and Dad were older than any of my friends' parents, as they had both been in their forties when I was born and had led full and unusual lives before coming to settle in England.

My father had been born in Sydney, a fourth-generation

Australian, and had trained in the family business to become a tent-maker. Later, he and his brother had built a circus tent of their own and had taken to the road with their show, Silvers Circus.

Mum, on the other hand, had been born in London. Her family emigrated to Australia when she was eleven, so she grew up in Perth but returned to England, aged sixteen, determined to become a writer. She worked in Fleet Street during the Blitz. Then, when she was in her thirties, she went back to Australia to find material to use in her books.

While travelling through the Nullarbor Plain, her car had broken down, and she had been rescued by my father, who was crossing the country with his circus.

After a whirlwind romance, they married and, a year later, my brother, David, was born.

Mum told me once that the months after David's birth were the happiest she ever knew. She had found the love of her life and a bright future lay ahead of them.

Sadly, her idyll was short-lived.

Out of the blue, Dad was struck down by a mystery illness. The doctors could not agree what the problem was, only that he had contracted a viral infection of the brain, probably a form of meningitis.

At first, it seemed he would not survive, but when, with customary stubbornness, he refused to die, my mother was warned he would be left with brain damage and would never be able to work again.

With a baby and an invalid husband to care for, Mum decided to return home to England. As a child, she had lived in the East End of London but, rather than return to the bustle of the capital, she felt the slower pace of life in Devon might help Dad's recovery and so the family settled in Exeter.

Against all the doctors' predictions, Dad's health slowly

returned and, as he grew stronger, he began to think of ways to earn a living.

There were few opportunities for circus owners in Devon at that time, so he decided instead to set up a business as a silk-screen printer. Neither he nor Mum knew much about printing, but Dad got a book from the local library and built the printing tables, screens and drying racks himself.

A couple of years later, I was born and for the next twenty years, the printing business supported our family.

Me, as a toddler, with (from the left) Dad, Mum and Granny. The photo was taken by my brother David on his brand new Box Brownie camera.

Although he always worked long hours, Dad never fully recovered from the effects of his illness. He suffered from headaches, sometimes lasting for days, which were so severe they left him partially paralysed and unable to speak. On more than one occasion, he collapsed over the printing table. Despite these setbacks, Dad would never give in and, as soon as his head cleared, and usually sooner than my mother wanted, he would return to work.

My father could never, in any way, be described as average. He was a big bear of a man with a warm heart and an infectious laugh who could find the humour in even the most difficult situations. Naturally quiet, he was one of life's observers, which meant that few people realised he had an unusual ambition.

As a teenager, he had spent his days training in his father's tent-making factory, designing and making tents for the biggest circuses in Australia, but, in his spare time, he had built a tent of his own. It was a scale model, perfect in every detail, a miniature replica of a circus big top, and he brought it with him to England, locked away in a trunk, in the hope that one day he would be able to finish it.

~

Yes, my parents were different, and in some ways, I think I was different, too.

I found it hard to fit in at school because I never seemed to have anything in common with the other children. I wanted to be friends with them, but I had no idea how to do it.

My classmates seemed to know instinctively how to start conversations or join in with games, but I never learned their secret and always ended up on my own watching everything from a distance.

It wasn't that I didn't like the other children. It was just that they seemed strange to me. They enjoyed things I didn't understand, like music and sport.

Many of our lessons involved songs, and the other children seemed genuinely to enjoy them. They would shriek with delight whenever a teacher pulled open the instrument store, but the sight of a box filled with tambourines and bongo drums made my heart sink.

I worried there must be something wrong with me and wondered if I was really the only person in the world who didn't like music.

I can still remember how excited I felt on my first day at Stoke Hill Junior School. I was seven years old and was already a confident reader. My favourite subject was maths and Mum had helped me learn my multiplication tables by heart, so I knew I was ready to start my formal education.

Stoke Hill was considered a progressive school. The newly completed buildings were bright and welcoming and stood high on a hill, surrounded by tarmac playgrounds and grass sports fields. The corridors and classrooms were painted in cheerful pastel colours, and huge windows allowed daylight to flood into every corner.

It was one of the first schools in Devon to try out a new form of child-led learning where pupils were allowed to work at their own rate instead of having all the class follow the same lesson. At the time, it was considered a radical approach to education, and we had regular visits from assessors to see how the new system was progressing.

Each morning our teacher handed out work cards to the class which were supposed to keep us busy until playtime. Some of the children became bored quite quickly and were allowed to change to activity-based tasks such as weighing sand with scales or making plasticine sculptures, but I was perfectly happy sitting at a table completing my work as neatly as I could. As soon as I finished a card, I would return it to the teacher and ask for another one.

It wasn't long before I finished all the cards in the box and the teacher told me I would have to wait for the others to catch up with me before we could all move on to a new set.

The next day I asked if I could start the new work cards yet, but my teacher told me I would have to wait. She suggested I read a book from the pile in the corner, but I explained that I had already read them all.

I asked again the next day, and the next day, and the next, until, finally, my teacher suggested I bring a book from home to read. She seemed surprised when I arrived with a copy of Collins Guide to European Butterflies and a dictionary in case there were any words I didn't understand.

I don't think she expected me to enjoy the book, but I loved it and read it from cover to cover several times, trying hard to memorise all the information.

By then, I had come to the conclusion that my classmates were not very bright. They didn't seem interested in lessons at all and only wanted to run around the playground screaming.

For me, playtime was the worst part of the day. I disliked it intensely. It was noisy, disorganised, and frightening. Worst of all, when I begged the teachers to let me stay inside and read, they told me that standing on my own, shivering, in the playground while they sat in a warm staff room drinking coffee, was good for me.

I began to think my teachers weren't very bright, either.

Me with my big brother David.

My brother, David, is seven years older than me and we were always inseparable. When Dad was ill and Mum was preoccupied looking after him, it was David who kept me busy.

He would push me around the garden in his go-kart, make tents out of blankets, or teach me how to wage war with his toy soldiers.

On the weekend, David and his friends were allowed to go to Saturday Morning Picture Club at the local cinema where they enjoyed cartoons, children's films and serials like The Perils of Pauline, where each episode ended with the heroine tied to a railway track or about to fall off a cliff.

Every Saturday, David begged to be allowed to take his little sister to the cinema with him, and I screamed at being left behind, until eventually, I became the youngest member of the club and was allowed to spend three hours a week staring at the screen with the big boys.

During the week, particularly during the holidays, David and I would act out our favourite scenes and, as I got older, we began to make up our own stories. We wanted to shoot films ourselves and dreamed of travelling the world and making movies in wonderful, exotic locations.

For a special treat, my parents took me to see Disney's Snow White at the cinema. I hated it, mainly because the wicked stepmother reminded me of my grandmother.

Of course, Granny was not tall or beautiful or magical. but she was exceptionally vain and jealous and treated my mother in much the same way that the wicked stepmother treated Snow White.

When the wicked stepmother transformed herself into an old lady and set out with her poisoned apple, I screamed so much that my mother had to take me out of the cinema.

Mum and Granny

One of my earliest memories is of hiding under a sofa while my grandmother screamed and shouted. I can remember burying my face in the carpet and shaking. I was absolutely terrified of her and, as I grew older, my fear turned into a deep loathing.

As a child, I didn't understand why Granny was so horrible to everyone. Even when she was trying to be nice, there was a coldness about her that drained the happiness from a room the moment she walked into it.

As an adult, I came to understand that she was a deeply unhappy woman who had been shaped by her life experiences. Intelligent and talented, she had been born into extreme poverty in the East End of London. Her mother had refused to let her go to school and had kept her at home to help with the housework and to look after her younger siblings.

When the school inspector arrived on the doorstep, Granny had been made to hide in a cupboard while her mother pretended that she had been taken ill with scarlet fever and had been sent to live with relatives in Brighton.

As she grew up, Granny had rebelled and found herself married with two young children while still in her teens.

She was clever and articulate but, barely able to read or write and with a young family to support, Granny spent her life scrubbing other people's floors or washing up in pubs and became bitter and resentful.

She took pride in the fact that she never made friends, but had a long list of enemies.

I think she was jealous of my mother because she saw in her a vision of how her life could have been, if only she had had the same opportunities. As she grew older, Granny became manipulative, violent, and increasingly insensitive to other people's feelings.

I didn't know until many years later, but when my mother was six months pregnant with me, my grandmother tried to push her down a flight of stairs. Fortunately, Mum had managed to catch hold of the bannister, and neither she nor I were hurt.

Granny insisted it had been an accident but my mother didn't believe her and, after that, my father had to make sure the two women were never left alone in the house together.

Dad told me once that he had begged Mum to walk out, but she had refused to leave, fearing that if she went, Granny would have been unable to cope on her own and would have ended up getting herself arrested.

It was probably the stress of living with Granny that led to my mother having a nervous breakdown when I was born.

My brother often teased me that I was so ugly that Mum took one look at me and collapsed.

Dad simply told me that Mummy had been very tired when I arrived and the doctors had put us into special rooms so that she could have plenty of rest.

When I grew up, Mum explained that, as she had recently arrived from Australia, her doctors had assumed that she had some strange tropical disease and, immediately after my birth, both she and I had been put into separate rooms in the isolation unit. For the first week of my life, she had not been allowed to touch me as I lay in a sterile box tended only by nurses wearing masks and thick rubber gloves.

Perhaps that was where I learned to enjoy being on my own.

My brother is dyslexic. Or rather, he is dyslexic now. When he was a child, he was just stupid and lazy, at least, that was what his teachers called him.

Back then, no one had heard of dyslexia, but Mum was convinced there must be a reason for David's inability to read or write.

For years, she wrote to every educational expert she could find and sent letters to newspapers and universities. Eventually, she discovered a professor who was researching "wordblindness" and, as a result, David was the first child in Devon to be officially diagnosed as dyslexic.

By then, he was fifteen and his teachers refused to believe that such a condition existed.

He left school with no formal qualifications, having endured years of being told he was retarded, when in reality, he was intelligent, talented and creative.

My mother never believed there was anything wrong with David. She knew he had gifts and abilities and devoted her life to helping him learn.

Every afternoon, as soon as he returned from school, she would make him go through the same list of spellings day after day after day, in the hope that they would finally stick in his memory.

I always enjoyed lessons and one day, when I was about six and David was thirteen, I asked if I could join in.

Mum gave me a piece of paper and, as she read out the words, I wrote them down in large, round letters.

Then, as Mum corrected David's work, I carefully ticked the words off my list.

"Look," I squealed, "I got them all right!"

I had expected them to be pleased.

Instead, David leaped to his feet and tore his paper to shreds.

"I'm not doing this anymore!" he shouted. "It's useless. I'm rubbish, aren't I? I'm never going to be any good at anything!"

The door slammed as he ran out of the room and I realised, for the first time, that doing well in tests doesn't make you popular.

In the sixties, eating disorders had not been invented.

The memories of wartime rationing were still fresh in people's memories and it was considered a sin to waste food.

Milk arrived on our doorstep each day in glass bottles. The tops were sealed by shiny foil tops that glistened in the morning sunlight and proved irresistible to blue tits.

Every morning, as soon as she came downstairs, Mum would hurry to the front door and carry the milk bottles through to the kitchen. Usually the foil bottle tops would have dents where the blue tits had been pecking at them with their sharp black beaks, and occasionally there would be a tear where a bird had broken through to the creamy milk beneath.

Often, the bottles were smeared with bird droppings and Mum always rinsed them carefully under the tap before putting them in the fridge.

As I watched her, I worried that some of the droppings might have got into the milk. What if the birds had poo on their claws, as they hopped around on the foil?

Soon my mind associated milk with bird droppings. I didn't want to upset Mum by explaining, so I stopped drinking milk. Every time she put a glass in front of me, I sat staring at it, sometimes for hours, as my mother encouraged or scolded me.

I thought if I waited for long enough, Mum would give in and take the milk away, but she never did.

Day after day, she would plonk a full glass in front of me and the battle of wills would begin. Sometimes I cried, sometimes I begged her to take it away, but mainly I just sat silently staring at the glass, trying to spot traces of bird poo floating in the whiteness.

It was not long before I realised food might contain unpleasant substances too. I studied the Weetabix that was waiting for me each morning and decided some of the smooth flakes of wheat looked suspiciously like insect wings.

I told Mum I didn't feel hungry and I wouldn't need any breakfast in the future.

I stopped drinking tea because, in the days before tea bags, the tea leaves looked like drowned flies.

Fruit juice was rejected because it had "bits" in it and soon I would only drink water.

I refused to eat brown bread and became suspicious of anything that might have dirt hidden in it. I even spread mashed potato across my plate to check it was untainted before I eating it.

I sensed that my behaviour was upsetting my mother. She sat by me for hours at mealtimes, insisting I couldn't leave the table until I had eaten something, but she never lost her temper or shouted at me.

Granny wasn't so patient. One night, when Dad was ill and Mum was upstairs looking after him, I can remember her plopping a bowl of rice pudding down in front of me and insisting that I eat it.

When I refused, she took a spoon and tried to force the rice pudding into my mouth. I spat it out, but she simply scraped the rice up from the tablecloth and shovelled it back into my mouth.

I tried to protest, but she stood behind me, the spoon clamped in her right hand, while her left arm wrapped across my chest, pinning my arms to my sides.

I wriggled and squirmed and choked as she forced the sweet, creamy pudding into my mouth and felt myself retching as some of it slid down my throat.

Each time I swallowed, I tried to call out, but my protests were choked by another spoonful of rice.

Tears of indignation filled my eyes and frustration churned my stomach until, finally, with a horrible rasping sound, I vomited with such force that the returning rice pudding hit the bowl and splattered up all over Granny.

She gasped in shock and I seized the chance to wriggle free and race upstairs to the sanctuary of my bedroom.

I can remember lying on my bed crying as my grandmother's voice echoed up from downstairs.

After that, mealtimes became a misery.

I didn't want to upset my mother because she was always kind and patient with me, but I had absolutely no appetite. I never felt hungry, and the thought of eating tied my stomach in knots.

Dad tried to help by challenging me to races. Who could eat the most peas? Or finish their potato first? It didn't work.

At school, I was made to sit at the table, staring at an untouched plate of food, long after the other children had left. When the dinner ladies wanted to clean the dining hall, I would be made to sit in the corridor outside the headmaster's office until the bell rang for afternoon lessons. This didn't worry me too much as it meant I avoided playtime, but I just wished everyone would leave me alone.

It was only when my mother took me to see the doctor that I realised things were getting out of hand.

The doctor weighed and measured me, then made me strip down to my knickers before poking my stomach and tutting at my protruding ribs and hipbones.

"Why won't you eat the meals your Mummy cooks for you?" he asked.

I knew he wouldn't understand, so I sat silently staring down at my shoes.

He repeated the question, but I didn't have an answer for him.

"There is nothing wrong with you, is there?" he said at last. "You're just being silly."

I looked up, but he was frowning, and I let my eyes drop back to my shoes.

"Your mummy and daddy are very worried about you.

You don't weigh nearly as much as you should do at your age."

I pressed my back against the chair and began to fidget nervously.

"There is only one answer." The doctor's voice was loud and resolute. "If you don't start eating properly, I will have to send some nurses to your house to take you away and put you in a special hospital. You won't be allowed to go home and you won't see your mummy and daddy again until you learn to do as you're told and eat what you're given. Do you understand?"

Fear gripped me and I blinked back tears as I nodded.

"Good. Remember, I have lots of seriously ill patients to look after and I don't want to waste my time talking to little girls who are being fussy about their food."

As I pulled on my coat, he turned to my mother.

"I think that should do the trick."

"Thank you, doctor," she replied gratefully.

As soon as we were out of the surgery, I burst into tears.

"You won't let the nurses take me away, will you?" I begged.

That night I tried hard to eat my evening meal, but the food seemed to grow in my mouth until I felt like a hamster with bulging cheek pouches. My throat had constricted to a tiny tube and the more I tried to swallow, the more I felt myself beginning to retch.

"She's playing up again," my grandmother said coldly. "Remember, dear, there are plenty of children in India that would be grateful for that food."

I wanted to tell her that the children in India were welcome to all my food, but I was afraid that if I opened my mouth, I would be sick across the table again.

It was Dad who took pity on me.

"This isn't doing any good," he said. "She ought to be in bed by now."

He watched as I cleaned my teeth and pulled on my pyjamas, then he tucked me into bed with his big hands and sat down beside me.

"Mummy's really worried about you."

"I know."

"Why won't you eat your food? She tries very hard to make nice things."

"I know," I repeated.

"Then what's the problem?"

He stroked my hair gently, and I knew he really wanted to understand.

"She mixes it all up," I said at last. "She puts it on the plate so it's all touching each other. I would eat some of it, like the mashed potatoes, but it's all mixed up with the cabbage."

"What's wrong with the cabbage?"

"It's not the cabbage…" I began hesitantly.

"Then what is it?"

I sniffed.

"It's the footprints."

"What footprints?"

I was silent for a long time and Dad kept stroking my hair as he waited.

"It's the things that live on the cabbage," I said at last. "It's the greenflies and the caterpillars. They leave footprints."

For a moment, he gazed at me, then his face broke into a grin.

"Are you telling me you won't eat your cabbage because you think greenflies have left footprints on it?"

He wrapped his arms around me, and I felt him shake with laughter.

"It's not funny," I protested. "They might have pooed on it too."

"They probably did," he agreed. "Greenflies do that sort of thing."

"Don't laugh at me!" I pounded his chest with my fists but, deep inside me, the tension eased.

"But you're the one who says funny things!"

"It's not funny, it's serious," I protested, but Dad tickled me.

"You're laughing!" he teased. "You mustn't laugh. This is serious."

"I know. It is serious," I insisted, but his laughter was infectious.

I wriggled away from him, but he went on tickling me until I shrieked with laughter. Finally, I leaned my head against his shoulder and knew I was safe.

"Please don't tell Mum about the cabbage. She wouldn't understand."

"No, I don't think she would," Dad agreed. "How about I ask her to keep the different foods separate on your plate? That way, you can eat the things that don't have footprints on them."

"Yes, please." I nodded. "And can I not have any gravy? It makes everything look like mud."

"Okay," he agreed. "I'll ask her."

He hugged me tightly, and I knew then he would never let the nurses take me away.

"I love you, Dad," I whispered.

Me aiming at tin cans in the garden

David was always mad about guns.

He had a huge collection of toy pistols and cowboy rifles and, as a toddler, I would trail behind him, pointing my finger and shouting "Bang!"

When David became a teenager, Dad bought him an air rifle, and I begged to be allowed to have a turn shooting at the row of battered Coke cans at the bottom of the garden.

The air rifle was much too heavy for me but I soon found that if I leaned the end of the barrel on the back of the garden bench and used two fingers to pull the trigger, I could send the cans flying as well as anyone else.

After that, whenever David had his friends around for a shooting competition, I would pester them to let me join in. They were reluctant at first, but eventually they gave in, and over the following years, I spent many happy hours firing lead pellets along the length of the garden.

I always found it hard to understand my mother's relationship with Granny.

"Do you really love her?" I asked one day as she scrubbed the collars of Dad's shirts with a bar of soap before putting them into the washing machine.

"Of course, I do," she replied. "She's my mummy."

"But that's not a reason."

"Yes, it is," Mum said firmly. "It's a daughter's duty to love her mother."

"I'll bet it was Granny who told you that."

Mum stopped scrubbing and looked at me in surprise.

"And why doesn't it work the other way around?" I went on. "What about a mother's duty to be loveable? I mean, I don't love you just because you're my mother. I love you because you're nice to me."

"So, if I stopped being nice to you, would you stop loving me?" she asked.

"Of course, I would," I said bluntly, "and I'm not going to love Granny just because she's my grandmother. I hate her because she's horrible to everyone. Nobody has the right to shout at people like she does."

Mum blinked quickly as she started scrubbing again.

"That's enough," she said. "I think it's time you went and played in the garden."

I knew Granny and Granddad had lived with us when I was a baby and I wondered why they had moved into a little flat of their own. When I asked David what had happened, he seemed reluctant to tell me but, after a little nagging, he gave in.

"There was a fight," he said. "You would have been about two at the time. It was worse than usual and Granny ended up smashing everything. When Dad tried to stop her, she bit his hand so hard he had to go to hospital and have seventeen stitches put in it."

"That must have hurt."

"Yes, I expect it did," he agreed. "The doctors came and saw Granny and said they wanted to put her into a special hospital, but Granddad wouldn't sign the papers."

"Why not?"

"Because she would only have been there for a while. Granddad said if they did that, Granny would kill him when she came out, so he wouldn't sign. That's when Dad said we had to leave and move here."

"Good," I said. "I'm glad we left, but I wish we had taken Granddad with us."

~

By the time I started junior school, Mum had made peace with Granny. She and Granddad visited us every week, and I often spent time with them during the holidays.

As the first day of term approached, Granny gave me some advice.

"Remember, dear," she said sternly, "I'm sure you will find it very frightening when you start at the big school, but there's one thing you must remember."

I looked up at her and she considered me for a moment before she went on.

"Whatever happens, you must hold your head up high and pretend you're as good as everyone else. That's what I do."

It seemed to make sense at the time and I think, for once, she was genuinely trying to be helpful, but now, as I look back, I can see the flaw in her logic and understand how much it said about her life.

~

Despite being a happy child, I was always fascinated by death.

When I was seven, my Uncle George was killed in a car crash. I can remember being woken in the middle of the night by the noise of a police officer banging on the front door to tell my mother that her brother was in critical condition in hospital.

The strange thing was that Mum and George had been estranged for years but, in the weeks before his death, she had been haunted by premonitions that something was going to happen to him. She had even taken to reading the obituaries in the local paper to check for his name.

After his funeral, I found myself thinking a lot about what it would be like to die.

Mum and Dad wouldn't answer my questions, and I wasn't convinced that David knew any more about the subject than I did.

I tried asking Granny, but she only burst into tears and told me I was an unfeeling brat.

I didn't understand why she was so upset that Uncle George had gone to heaven. The description I had heard from my mother made heaven sound wonderful. No school, no food, no arguments. Nothing to do but play all day and talk to Jesus.

Yes, heaven sounded wonderful and I couldn't understand why everyone didn't want to go there straight away. Soon, I began wondering how people actually got to heaven.

You had to die, of course, but I didn't know exactly what dying meant. I had heard about people passing over, or going through the gateway, or slipping away from this world, but none of those phrases made sense to me.

I knew people could die by being strangled, or stabbed, or drowned, or burned, or run over by a car, but I longed to know how it felt to go through that ultimate transition and arrive in paradise. I knew there would be pain involved, but that didn't discourage me at all.

In my mind, dying seemed very exciting.

Eventually, I decided that if no one would explain how death worked, I would try to find out for myself. It didn't make any sense to me to spend years coping with school, eating and having to talk to people, if heaven was really so much better.

A few days later, my mother found me laying in the road near our house waiting for a car to catapult me to heaven. Luckily, I had chosen a quiet backstreet and all the drivers had managed to avoid me.

With hindsight, it seems strange that no one had stopped to find out why a small girl was lying in the middle of the road. Apparently, one of my classmates' parents had recognised me and summoned my mother.

I had never seen my mother cry before.

It had not occurred to me she might be upset by my plan and I tried to explain that I had not meant to make her sad, but she just kept weeping and asking me to promise never to do such a thing again.

Dad arrived soon afterwards and his face was so grey that I knew he was about to slide into another headache. I promised I would never try to get myself run over again and felt genuinely sorry for the upset I had caused.

But it did not change the way I felt about death. It still seemed like a great adventure, and I couldn't wait to experience it. However, to avoid upsetting anyone, I decided to delay my next attempt until both my parents were safe in heaven, waiting for me.

I always felt sorry for Granddad. He was a tiny man with worried eyes and a shiny bald head, and I knew he was as frightened of Granny as I was. Sometimes he would take me shopping with him and we would have to walk from one end of Exeter to the other to find shops that would serve him. Most of the butchers and greengrocers had banned him because of the number of times Granny had complained about what he had bought and had made him take things back.

When Uncle George died, Granny was heartbroken, but her reaction, three years later, when Granddad died, was very different.

As usual, Granddad had been sent out with a long shopping list, but he had suffered a heart attack in the street and had been taken to hospital in an ambulance. By the time Granny got there, he was already dead.

Shortly afterwards, Granny arrived on our doorstep and, as Mum opened the door, her first words were, "Your father's gone and died and he hasn't even signed his pension book. His pension's due tomorrow, so that means I'm going to lose a week's money. He always was an inconsiderate man."

I begged to be allowed to go to Granddad's funeral, but Mum wouldn't hear of it. She said that my headmaster wouldn't give permission for me to miss school, but I am sure that she never even asked him. I think she was afraid I would start thinking about death again.

As soon as the funeral was over, Granny packed all Granddad's clothes into bags and arranged for them to be taken to the tip. Then she began visiting second-hand shops and selling her jewellery and knick-knacks.

"Don't you want them anymore?" I asked innocently.

"Not where I'm going," she answered.

"Where's that?"

"A long way away where no one will have to worry about me."

I knew better than to pester Granny when she was in a mood, so I waited until later and repeated her words to David.

"What do you think she meant?"

"No idea." He wrinkled his nose. "Maybe she's going to kill herself."

"I hope not." I said earnestly.

"Really?" David looked at me in surprise. "I thought you hated her."

"I do," I agreed, "but it wouldn't be fair on Granddad. Not yet. He deserves some time in heaven on his own."

A few weeks later, I returned from school to find Mum crying and Dad sitting with his head in his hands.

"What's wrong?" I asked in alarm.

"It's all right." Dad reassured me. "It's your grandmother. She's going on a trip and Mum's a bit worried about her."

"What sort of a trip?" I asked.

"She's going back to Australia," Mum blurted. "She says she's going to find herself a new husband."

"Really? That's great!"

"No, it isn't!" Mum burst into a new flood of tears. "She's going to get herself into all sorts of trouble, and I won't be there to get her out of it."

"We can't stop her," Dad said tiredly. "She's sane. At least the doctors say she is, and she's managed to raise enough money for the journey. Her sisters will have to look after her once she gets there."

He put his arm around Mum's shoulder and kissed her hair.

"Maybe it will all work out for the best."

"No." Mum's voice was pitiful. "It's going to end in disaster. I know it."

David was as happy as me when he heard the news. He had just passed his driving test and offered to drive Granny to Southampton, where she was due to board her ship.

"It's brilliant!" he grinned. "She can catch herself some

rich old sheep farmer and we won't ever have to see her again. Thank you, God!"

Eventually, Dad convinced Mum she couldn't stop Granny from leaving, so instead, Mum focused her attention on getting everything ready for the trip.

For weeks, our lives revolved around Granny. Mum took her out for countless shopping trips, to appointments with the hairdresser, chiropodist, dentist, or to have her inoculations.

The contents of her flat had to be sorted and packed and the furniture taken to the auction rooms to be sold. Granny insisted on spending every penny she had on new clothes. There were evening gowns, day dresses, high-heeled sandals and even an emerald-green swimming costume with white lacing.

When Mum tried to persuade her to save some cash for an emergency, Granny ridiculed her. She was certain that, once she found her new man, money wouldn't be a problem.

When the day of Granny's departure arrived, Dad and David took it in turns to drive the car to Southampton. Granny sat, squeezed between Mum and me, on the back seat, wearing an enormous black hat with a wide brim to protect her complexion from the Australian sun. It was a long journey.

Finally, we arrived at the port, and Dad found a trolley. He wheeled Granny's trunk to the departure hall, and she tottered behind him while Mum, David and I pulled the rest of the luggage from the boot.

By the time we had carried everything into the departure hall, Granny was nowhere to be seen.

"She's gone to check out her cabin," Dad said. "I expect she'll be back in a minute."

A porter took away the rest of her luggage and we sat down to wait.

An hour later, an announcement told us that the gang

planks were being removed so we went out onto the harbourside.

I was awed by the size of the liner. It loomed over us like a tower block, all shining paint and chrome railings. Excited travellers leaned down, waving their farewells to friends and families standing around us.

Mum shielded her eyes with her hand as she tried to pick out Granny among the faces high above us.

But she was not there.

Thirty minutes later, with a blare of sirens and a huge churning of seawater, the mighty vessel slid away from the dock and headed out to sea.

Mum stood for a long time, watching it go.

"I thought she might at least have waved goodbye," she said at last.

CHAPTER 2

When Granny left, Mum was quiet and withdrawn, but Dad was in a boisterous mood. After work, he played games with me, kicking a football around in the garden or whacking a tennis ball with badminton racquets. It was then that he first mentioned the model circus.

Dad in the early 1930s with the canvas tents of his model circus.

I was eleven by then, and David would have been eighteen. We were both fascinated and insisted Dad took us up to the attic at once so we could see the tent that had been hidden away for so long. I suppose I was expecting some sort of toy like the model farm I had in my bedroom.

What I had not expected was the size of the tents. There were two of them, a big top and a menagerie. Dad explained the menagerie was the tent where the circus people kept all their animals.

The menagerie alone was nearly two and a half metres long.

Reluctantly, Mum agreed we could use the dining room to erect it. Dad brought in a large sheet of plywood, which he laid over two trestles, and the rest of the day was spent hammering in miniature tent pegs, splicing sections of tent together and learning how to erect a proper circus tent.

Finally, the tent was up, and David and I were delighted. It was perfect. Magical. Every rope, every splice, every tent pole was a tiny replica of the real thing.

"Can we put up the big top now?" I asked excitedly, but Mum would not hear of it.

"It's too late. It's nearly midnight already. Tomorrow's Sunday. You can spend the whole day working on the circus if you want to."

We did want to. We were entranced. Dad pointed out that the big top was considerably bigger than the menagerie. The only way of fitting both tents into the dining room would be to dismantle the table and take the chairs and sideboard into the hall.

"What!" Mum was outraged, but she was also outvoted. The rest of us were unconcerned. After all, we could always eat our meals in the kitchen for a few days. The appeal of the circus was just too great.

Dad explained he had always wanted to bring the circus to life and fill it with tiny moving figures of acrobats, jugglers and clowns. He wanted to make a mechanism for each figure so the horses would gallop around the ring, the band would lift their instruments, and in the centre ring, lions, tigers and even an elephant would all move.

David and I were hooked. Dad's dream became our dream. Mum had been right to be concerned. It would be ten years before the table returned to the dining room.

David might have struggled to put words down on paper, but he loved telling stories. He had a gift for seeing the absurdity of life and was always ready to share his thoughts with any audience he could find.

Every time he went to the corner shop, he would come home and act out the incredible things that had happened to him on the way. He exaggerated, of course. We knew him too well to believe his stories, but they always made us laugh.

If he had been born twenty years later, he would probably have become a stand-up comedian.

When the Northcott Theatre in Exeter opened a youth club, Mum enrolled David as a founder member. It was a brilliant move. Finally, he found a place where his creativity and artistic talents were recognised.

Dyslexia made it difficult for him to read scripts, but he had a wonderful memory which gave him a great advantage.

He found he loved working backstage too, and his inventive nature and the practical skills that Dad had taught him made him an ideal choice as a stage manager or set designer.

I listened avidly to David's stories about the theatre youth club and, to my parents' surprise, I asked if I could join the junior section. It was the first time I had ever asked to do anything outside home and they agreed to let me give it a go.

I nearly changed my mind on the first evening when I pushed open the door to the clubroom and was confronted by a dozen children running around screaming.

Fortunately, a bouncy young woman in a rainbow-coloured leotard, pink leggings and purple leg warmers spotted me and made me feel welcome. She explained the others were warming up before the main session began and were using their imaginations to pretend to be lions, dogs, elephants or any other kind of animal they chose.

I had never experienced anything like it, and I was excited. I decided to be a monkey and, moments later, I was so busy climbing over chairs and making monkey noises that I hardly noticed the music pumping from speakers at either end of the room.

I loved the club, and I adored acting. It was wonderful. I could be anyone or anything I wanted to be. For the first time in my life, I found somewhere I belonged. I wasn't greatly interested in the other children, but I felt a huge bond with the adults running the classes and I decided that, one day, I would become an actress.

I didn't tell anyone that I wanted to act. Not even Dad. Everyone thought of me as the quiet one of the family, and I was convinced they wouldn't understand.

~

After school and at weekends, Dad taught David and me about model making so that we could help him with the miniature circus. I don't mean that he taught us how to assemble models, like the plane and car kits that were so popular in the 1970s, but instead, he taught us the skills we would need to make models from scratch.

We learned to carve, solder and splice. After a while, even Mum accepted the loss of her dining room and joined the team.

Dad was the mastermind who knew exactly how the finished model would work, but we were each given our own tasks to complete. I can vividly remember landscaping the surface of the platform that the tents would stand on, gluing down sawdust before painting it to look like grass and making tiny flowers beds around the caravan section with hand-painted plants cut out of paper.

~

In the final year of primary school, we all had to sit the eleven-plus exam.

Many of the children in my class were worried about it. Their parents made them go to special clubs to help them with "exam awareness" and some even had private tutors that came to their houses after school.

My parents never mentioned the eleven-plus, and I didn't really understand what all the fuss was about. I overheard one boy saying his father had warned him that, if he didn't pass the exam, he would have to spend his life clearing drains and some of the girls boasted they had been promised bicycles if they passed and got into the grammar school. I wanted to know what a grammar school was, but I didn't like to ask.

One morning, a large white envelope arrived in the post and I could tell from my mother's reaction that it was something important. I watched as she pulled out a crisp, neatly folded letter and read it carefully. Then she folded it up, put it in her pocket and went out of the room.

A few minutes later, she was back with Dad beside her. They looked at me with strange expressions and I began to wonder if I had done something wrong.

"What is it?" I asked.

"Do you remember the test you took at school?" Mum began.

"The eleven-plus exam?"

"Yes."

"Did I pass?"

"You did more than that," Dad grinned. "You've won a scholarship!"

I looked at him blankly.

"We're very proud of you." Mum beamed.

"But what does it mean?"

"It means you'll be going to a school called Maynards," she told me. "It's a very special school for girls here in Exeter and they only take pupils who are very clever. Being chosen is a real honour."

Suddenly, she engulfed me in a massive hug and squeezed me so tight I could hardly breathe.

"They're going to send a list of uniform and all the things you'll need." Dad's voice was muffled as Mum's arms were still firmly around my ears.

"And you're going to do hockey as well. That will be fun." I wriggled out of my mother's embrace and filled my lungs. "Now, off you go to school and tell all your friends."

I didn't tell anyone at school about my scholarship because nobody asked me.

Most of the children seemed excited about their own results, but some were sitting at their desks crying and quite a few were absent.

Everyone else in my class was going to the grammar school or the secondary modern school, which was also known as the comprehensive. Children who were inseparable best friends found they were about to be divided. Some vowed to remain besties for life, but many sensed that nothing would ever be the same again.

No one could have told from my mother's voice that she had been born a Cockney in the East End of London and had grown up in an Australia.

I suspect that while she was working in Fleet Street during the war, she made an effort to cultivate a "BBC" accent, which was considered very sophisticated at the time. She always spoke with precise, cultured tones that sounded rather upper class.

In Exeter, where most people still had strong Devonian accents, she sounded almost foreign, and her hair, which was curled every morning into the same style as the Queen, made her look distinctly aristocratic.

She always took great care of her appearance and was very proud of a tall dressing mirror which stood in the corner of her bedroom. She told me once that the difference between an Englishwoman and a Frenchwoman was that the Englishwoman would use a hand mirror to put on her makeup, whereas a Frenchwoman would use a full-length mirror to check her entire outfit before leaving the house.

Looking back, my lack of interest in fashion and my habit of dressing in jeans and floppy jumpers must have been a great disappointment to her.

But I may be wrong. She may not have cultivated her sophisticated voice intentionally. Mum always had a strange type of osmosis that allowed her to soak up accents from the people around her. When we went on holiday to Scotland, David and I were intrigued to hear how her vowels softened and her speech gained a wonderfully highland lilt. Whenever we visited Wales, her voice soon undulated with the melodious rhythms of the valleys. We often teased her about her changing accent, but Mum always insisted we were imagining it.

Unfortunately, we were not the only ones to notice.

In the last week of the summer term, Stoke Hill School always held a summer fete. Exeter was not culturally diverse in the 1970s and it was unusual to see anything other than white faces around the city, but we did have one Sikh family living at the end of our street.

Teesha Singh was in my class and she was as quiet as me. We were not really friends as we were both too shy to talk to each other, but the teachers often sat us at the same table so we could be quiet together.

As Mum and I walked around the stalls at the fete, Mum saw Teesha and her mother by the refreshment tent.

"Isn't that one of your friends?" Mum asked.

She didn't wait for me to reply, but headed straight across and began talking to Teesha's mother.

Normally, pupils had to wear grey and green school uniforms, but we had been allowed to wear our home clothes for the afternoon.

Teesha wore a wonderful outfit of ankle-length turquoise velvet and embroidered silk. She seemed self-conscious, and I guessed she would rather have been wearing a miniskirt and tank top, like the other girls, but I couldn't help but envy the exotic splendour of her clothes.

I was admiring the large glass rubies decorating her sandals when I noticed Mum's voice.

"Oh, my goodness, that really is most wonderful."

My eyes shot to Teesha's mother's face and my heart sank. It was clear from her flushed cheeks and tight lips that she could hear the unnatural lilt too.

I cringed as Mum chattered on in an accent that made the hairs on the back of my neck stand up with shame.

Finally, Teesha's mother drew herself up to her full height, bowed her head and walked away.

"How could you do that?" I demanded as soon as she had gone. "She thought you were mocking her!"

"Don't be ridiculous, dear. Why would she think that?"

"Because you were copying her accent!"

"No, I wasn't," Mum said indignantly. "I would never do such a thing. That would be extremely rude."

In the last week of August, a letter arrived from Maynards. It had been signed by the headmistress herself, and there were several pages of detailed notes about the items I would need for each lesson and a plan of the buildings to help me find my way around.

It was very exciting, and I studied the plan intently, determined to memorise every detail.

"That's a shame."

Mum was still reading the letter.

"What is?" I asked.

"It says here that pupils are not encouraged to take part in any clubs or activities outside of school. They mean things like Girl Guides and youth clubs."

"That's all right. I don't want to go to Girl Guides."

"It means you won't be able to go to Young Northcott any more. It says here that great importance is placed on homework and girls are expected to devote themselves entirely to their studies."

"But that's rubbish!" I protested. "Going to Young Northcott won't stop me doing homework."

"I know, love, I'm sorry. Maybe Maynards has its own drama club."

I could tell Mum was worried I would be nervous about my new school, because she made me go to bed early on the last night of the holidays and gave me a steaming mug of hot milk to help me sleep.

As I climbed into my pyjamas, she perched on the edge of

the bed and told me about the school she had attended in Australia and how much she had missed the children she left behind in London. She assured me I would make lots of new friends at Maynards.

When she kissed me goodnight and went downstairs, I then tiptoed to the bathroom and poured the milk down the loo.

Mum need not have worried about me. I was far more excited than I was nervous. I was going to study Latin, algebra, chemistry, and physics and have homework every night. What more could a girl want?

And I was in love with my new uniform. The crisp white blouse, tartan tunic and silky tie made me feel grown up. Even the regulation navy knickers that stretched up to my armpits and drooped to my knees didn't bother me.

I knew I was going to be happy at Maynards, and I was right. I loved the strict rules and rigid routines. No one was allowed to shout or run, even when they were outside. There was no such thing as playtime, only break, when pupils were allowed to let off a little steam by walking around the grounds.

The school itself was a magnificent example of Victorian gothic splendour. Compared with Stoke Hill, it felt ancient and solidly rooted in the past. The main building had been constructed from warm red brick with rows of imposing mullion windows, and high against the skyline, an intricate bell tower was topped by a weather-vane.

Inside, the corridors and classrooms were lined with dark wooden panelling and the floors were worn wooden boards that creaked or terracotta tiles that clicked with every step.

Instead of sitting at shared tables, each girl had her own desk, which was inspected daily. Mine was always immaculate, with textbooks piled on the left side, in size order, and subject books on the right. It made me ridiculously happy that the gap down the middle was the perfect size for my pencil case and geometry set.

There were thirty girls in my class and sixty in the year. On the first day of term, many of them seemed overawed by their new surroundings and, for once, my quietness did not make me stand out.

The teachers addressed us as "ladies" and expected us to behave as such. We were now Maynardians and must uphold the traditions and standards of our school.

We were each given a copy of the school song and were told to learn it as quickly as possible. When I saw the chorus was written in Latin, I thought my heart would burst with happiness.

Walking home, I wore my new leather satchel on my shoulder and a smile on my face.

As I reached the corner of my road, something thudded into my back. Turning, I heard a voice shout, "Snob!"

Behind me was a group of boys from Stoke Hill. They had been in the year below me, but I don't think they recognised me in my new uniform.

"Stuck-up snob!" one shouted as he bent down and scraped another handful of mud from the gutter.

I fled.

~

"Don't worry, dear, it will come off," Mum said as she sponged the mess off my blazer.

"What's a snob?"

She glanced at me but didn't answer.

"Those boys are stupid. They're just jealous."

"Why?"

"Some people don't like others being different from them. It's not your fault. You just have to stand up to them."

After that, I arrived home each day with mud splattered across my back and tears pricking my eyes.

David offered to "sort out" the boys for me, but I didn't want him to get into trouble.

One morning, there was a ring at the doorbell and Mum told me that she had arranged for two of my classmates, who lived near us, to walk to and from school with me. I was mortified.

As I opened the door, Jess and Amy smiled at me. I had noticed them sitting together in class, but I hadn't yet spoken to either of them.

"Hello, you're Diana, aren't you?" Amy asked brightly.

She was tall for her age, like me, with thick brown hair drawn back into ponytails. Jess was a little shorter and had sandy-coloured plaits. Both of them blinked at me from behind large round glasses and I was reminded of a pair of owls.

Pulling on my blazer, I closed the door behind me, before Mum had a chance to give me her usual morning hug and kiss goodbye.

"Amy says you've been having trouble with the little oiks from the council estate," Jess began. "Is that right?"

"Sort of…" I said hesitantly.

"Us too," Jess agreed. "Little bastards."

I glanced sideways at her. I had never heard anyone use the word before.

"Sometimes, they throw stuff at me," I admitted.

"And what do you do?"

"Do? Nothing… I just go home."

"Really?" Amy looked disappointed.

"My mother says it's best to ignore them," I said lamely.

"One of them tried to pull Jess's plaits yesterday." Amy grinned. "You should have heard her. She told him that if he ever came near her again, she would remove his spleen with her hockey stick."

They both dissolved into giggles.

"I don't think he even knew what a spleen was!" Jess spluttered.

"No," Amy laughed, "but then, neither do I!"

To my surprise, Jess and Amy didn't seem to mind walking to school with me. They were loud and self-confident and giggled a lot, but they asked me questions and actually listened to my answers.

They told me about their families, where they had been on holiday, and what they hoped to do when they left school.

It soon became clear that they had their entire lives mapped out. I was impressed. It had not even occurred to me that, one day, I would have to leave home, but Jess and Amy had already planned their future careers and decided which universities they were going to attend.

They were also very interested in boys. Whenever they saw a teenage boy in the street, they would pretend not to notice him, then burst into giggles when he had gone past.

I didn't get the joke, but I joined in, enjoying the novelty of being included. A strange thought popped into my head. Maybe, just maybe, I was finally starting to fit in.

As we approached the school gates, other girls were arriving from all directions. Many were delivered to school in gleaming cars, but a few arrived at the bus stop opposite the entrance.

"Do you know anything about Dawn?" Amy asked, pointing to a pale girl with startling ginger hair who was stepping off a bus.

I shook my head.

"Sara says she's a free girl."

"A what?" I asked.

"A free girl. You know. She's here on a scholarship because her parents can't afford the fees."

"Shhh!" Jess hissed at her. "You know we're not allowed to talk about it."

"About what?" I asked.

"About the scholarships," Jess whispered. "It was on the information sheets we were sent. Didn't your parents show you? Anyone caught talking about the free girls gets a detention."

"Why?"

"We're not allowed to treat them like oiks. We have to make them feel like they belong here."

"Oh, I see," I lowered my head to hide the flush burning my cheeks.

"Well, I'm sure Dawn's a free girl and we know Heather is…"

"Leave it!" Jess snapped. "Seriously, Amy, I'm not doing detention just because you can't keep your mouth shut!"

When lessons finished, Amy and Jess were waiting for me in the cloakrooms. They chatted and giggled all the way home and didn't notice that I had slipped back into my familiar silence.

"That's better, isn't it?" Mum smiled as she saw my mud-free blazer. "I knew things would be easier once you made some friends."

Progress on the circus was slow. We had all agreed that everything in our model had to be made by hand and so a single figure could take weeks or even months to complete.

First, Dad worked out the design on paper, then he built a skeleton from wire. Next, a wooden body would be carved to fit over the skeleton, and the face and hands moulded from paste.

Once the figure was complete, a mechanism was built using brass cogwheels and steel rods, and finally, when Dad was content that it moved as it should do, the figure was painted and a tiny outfit made to dress it.

As I said, progress was slow, but as time passed, we were encouraged by the reactions of friends and neighbours to our project. It seemed everyone who saw our circus loved it, and if they thought we were mad to devote so much time to a single model, they were all too polite to say so.

~

My hopes that there would be a drama club at Maynards were soon dashed. There were no after-school clubs at all. Instead, we were given several homework assignments each night, including weekends, and were expected to borrow books from the school library and write a report on each one when we finished it.

But while drama was not encouraged, singing was compulsory. Music was considered an essential subject for young ladies and, twice a week, we would trail across to the music room for lessons.

Mrs Mead, our music teacher, considered herself to be something of a free spirit. She wore brightly coloured scarves, pink lipstick and had once been seen with an artificial flower tucked behind her ear. It was clear that many of the other teachers disapproved of her and equally clear that Mrs Mead didn't care.

The music room was well away from the main classrooms, and lessons were the only opportunity pupils had to be as loud as they liked.

At the beginning of each lesson, Mrs Mead handed out song sheets and then settled herself down at the piano. The other girls loved the relaxed atmosphere and, as the weeks went by, I found myself relaxing, too. One day, as the voices rose around me, I joined in.

"No, no, no!" Mrs Mead stopped playing and swivelled the piano stool around to face us. "Who was that?"

Her eyes swept across the class.

"Someone is flat," she said accusingly. "Listen."

She tapped a piano key, and a note rang out.

"Middle C everyone."

The girls around me hit the note effortlessly.

"No, I can't hear it. One at a time, please."

She pointed at each girl in turn, tapped the piano key, and listened to their response. As her finger worked its way around the room, my heart pounded. Finally, she pointed at me. I had no choice but to open my mouth and sing.

"Oh, dear."

Mrs Mead made no attempt to conceal her disappointment.

"Don't laugh, girls," she scolded. "This is not funny. Come here."

As I walked to the front of the class, every eye fixed on me. My cheeks blazed and I felt a wild impulse to make a dash for the door, but instead, I stood self-consciously by the piano.

"Again." Mrs Mead instructed.

I tried. I really tried. Each time she struck the note, I let out a sound, but I had no idea what she wanted from me. The other girls seemed to know instinctively how to change their tone to match that of the piano, but I was completely lost. To me, the sound the piano was making and the sounds I could produce with my voice bore no relation to each other.

But Mrs Mead was not going to be beaten.

"Higher dear, you nearly had it then."

Ignoring the sniggers from behind me, I raised my voice until it squealed.

"No! Not like that. Listen to the piano. Feel the note, then open your mouth and let it flow out of you."

I tried again, and the sniggers grew louder.

"I can see this is going to some take time," Mrs Mead sighed. "You must come here at break time tomorrow. I'll soon have you singing like a lark.

The next day, when I reported to the music room, Mrs Mead wasted no time in getting started.

"We will begin with something simple," she said and played the tune Three Blind Mice.

"Right, off you go, dear."

She played the tune again, and I sang the words.

"I see. Perhaps we had better take it one note at a time."

Mrs Mead did not give in easily. Every Friday, for the rest of the term, I visited the music room and tried to hit the same notes. It was always Three Blind Mice.

On the last Friday of term, she smiled sadly at me.

"Never mind, dear, we did try, didn't we?"

I was used to Dad being ill, but it came as a surprise when Mum told me she would soon be going into hospital. She told me she needed to have a hysterectomy and explained that she would be in hospital for two weeks, and then, if everything went well, she would go to a convalescent home in the country for another two weeks.

Her tone was calm and reassuring, but I kept worrying that she wasn't telling me the whole truth. I asked Dad if he was sure Mum was going to be all right, but his expression did nothing to reassure me. I didn't know it then, but his mother had died while having the same operation when he was only a little older than me.

In the days before she went into hospital, Mum made sure everything was as prepared as possible. I helped her clean the house from top to bottom and watched as she checked the washing was up to date and the larder was full of packets of dried peas and mashed potatoes.

She left written instructions by the washing machine, iron, and fridge.

I didn't want to go to school on the day Mum was due at the hospital, but I knew it would upset her if I made a fuss.

"Don't worry dear," she said, as she hugged me goodbye, "Dad and David will look after you and I will be back in no time."

I wanted to hold on to her forever, but Jess and Amy were waiting at the door, so I gave her a quick kiss and tried to smile.

"I will come and visit you," I promised.

"Of course you will. I'm looking forward to it already."

I could tell Dad was worried about Mum, but he did his best to hide it. She had told him not to visit her immediately after the operation, as the doctors had warned it would take until the following morning for the anaesthetic to wear off, but he phoned to find out how things had gone and seemed satisfied with the doctor's report.

"It all sounds good. No complications and they say I can see her in the morning."

"Can I come too?" I asked.

"No, but I'll take you after school," he promised. "Now, go and change out of your uniform and I'll have your tea on the table."

I was in my bedroom pulling on a pair of jeans when I heard the front doorbell. I listened curiously and heard David's footsteps echo along the downstairs hall and the scrape of the front door being opened.

The voice was muffled, but I recognised it at once.

Grabbing a jumper, I raced out and peered down into the hall. There was no mistake. Granny stood there, wearing the enormous black hat she had taken to Australia. I wanted to find something heavy and drop it on her, but instead, I retreated to my room and finished getting dressed.

Granny had disappeared and David was struggling through the front door, weighed down with luggage, by the time I came downstairs.

"Why is she here?" I asked.

"God only knows. I thought we'd got rid of the old bitch."

"Diana!" Granny's voice called from the lounge. "Come here and give me a kiss."

Reluctantly, I went into the lounge. She seemed much smaller than I remembered. Her arms were held out towards me, but I did not move.

"I've brought presents," she said in a sing-song voice. "Presents for my favourite grandchildren."

"We're your only grandchildren."

Dad appeared from the kitchen with two plates of food, laid them on the table, then disappeared again without acknowledging Granny.

I'm not sure if she noticed him, but if she did, she didn't react.

"David," Granny beckoned to him, "bring that red case in here. The rest can go up to my room."

"Your room?"

"The spare room, dear. It will have to do for now."

David hesitated. His eyes caught mine, and I shrugged uncertainly.

"Are you staying here, then?" he asked.

"Of course, I am."

"No. I'm afraid that's not happening."

Dad stood in the doorway with two more plates.

"You're welcome to stay for a meal, but after that you'll have to go," he said firmly. "And I'm afraid there's not much food, as I was only cooking for three. I've spread it four ways, but there's plenty of bread and butter if anyone's still hungry."

David and I took our places at the table and waited for the explosion.

"I see." Granny's voice was icy. "I'm no longer welcome, is that it? I've travelled halfway around the world to be reunited with my family, and this is how I'm greeted?"

"We didn't know you were coming..." David began, but Granny cut across him.

"You're turning me out in the street? An old woman? With nowhere to go?"

"You can stay in a guesthouse tonight." Dad said. "I'll find a room somewhere."

"But I need to be with my family!" Granny wailed. "You're all I have in the world!"

"What about your sisters…" I asked, but Granny rounded on me.

"Don't mention those ingrates!" she screamed. "Money! That's all they're interested in! They thought I had a fortune, but once they found I've got nothing, they threw me out."

"Why did they think you had a fortune?" David asked.

"What did you want me to tell them?" she sobbed. "That I'm a poor, penniless widow, abandoned by her own kith and kin?"

"Nobody has aband—" Dad couldn't get the words out before she was off again.

"After all I've done for this family, you turn your backs on me in my hour of need!"

Her voice rose dramatically.

"Well, I won't burden you anymore. I'm off to the river. You'll all be happier when I'm gone!"

David looked shocked as she turned towards the door, but Dad's face was expressionless.

"I'm going!" Granny screeched. "You'll never see me again."

I felt I should do something, but I had no idea what.

"Keep your meal," she sobbed. "I won't need food where I'm going."

"Wait," I jumped up, but Dad caught my hand.

"Let her go," he said quietly.

"We can't!" I protested. "What will Mum say?"

Across the table, I could see David was as lost as I was. We listened as Granny's footsteps echoed along the hall and the front door slammed behind her.

"Should we call the police?" David asked.

I looked at Dad, but his face was white and I could see he was slipping deep into a headache. David and I helped him across to the sofa.

The minutes passed, and we looked at each other helplessly.

"I'm calling the police," David said at last. "We can't just let her drown herself."

As he dialled the number, the doorbell rang.

Pulling open the door, I found Granny on the doorstep, her hair glistening with raindrops.

Without a word, she leaned past me, pulled an umbrella from the stand and shook it open.

"Are you coming in?" I asked stupidly.

"Never!" she spat, and turned away.

~

"You don't think she'd really do anything silly, do you?" I asked Dad later.

"Of course not. Would she really be worried about getting wet if she meant to drown herself?"

"But what do we do now?" David asked. "We can't just go to bed."

He had already spent an hour driving around Exeter without finding any trace of Granny.

"We've notified the police," Dad reassured him. "There's really nothing else we can do tonight. I suggest we all try to get some sleep."

It was three o'clock in the morning when a policeman knocked on the door.

Bleary-eyed, I frowned at him. At his side, Granny smirked.

"This is my little granddaughter," she announced. "Diana, perhaps you can make this nice gentleman a cup of tea?"

I wanted to hit her. I didn't care if I was arrested. It would be worth it to vent the anger boiling inside me.

"You decided not to drown yourself, then?" I snapped and sensed a wave of disapproval from the policeman.

"Your grandmother tells me she lives here. Is that correct?"

"No."

"But she can stay for now." Dad was tying his dressing gown as he came downstairs. "It's too late for anything else tonight."

"Thank you, sir." The policeman sounded relieved. "In that case, I will leave you all to get some sleep. Good night, madam." He nodded at Granny and she smiled coyly back at him.

"Goodnight, officer."

She wiggled her fingers at him as he left.

David watched the performance from the bottom of the stairs.

"And now, perhaps you will take my cases up to my room," Granny ordered as she sailed past him.

I put the kettle on and Dad, David and I sat in the kitchen. The night had taken its toll and none of us felt like sleeping.

I had grown up with Granny, but I still couldn't make sense of her mercurial temperament. She had left the house threatening suicide and returned, hours later, flirting with a policeman.

"Do you know what I find hardest?" Dad asked.

"What?"

"Since she arrived, Granny's never once asked about your mother. I don't think she even noticed she's not here."

~

By the time Mum returned from the convalescent home, Dad had found a small flat on the other side of Exeter, and Granny had been moved in.

I was afraid the news of her unexpected return would upset Mum, but I think, deep down, she knew Granny would not stay away for long.

It had been nice while it lasted.

CHAPTER 3

I must have been in the third year at Maynards before I told Jess and Amy about the circus. I suppose I had been afraid they would laugh at me if I told them how I spent my free time, but one afternoon, on the way home, I suggested they come in and see it.

I don't know what they were expecting, but they followed me politely into the house, and when I showed them the big top with the multitude of figures we had created, the expressions on their faces were priceless.

"You made this?" Amy asked. "It's incredible. I've never seen anything like it."

"It was my dad, really. David and I have been helping him."

"It's awesome!" Jess was equally impressed. "I wish I had the patience to do something like that. It ought to be in a museum or something."

"What are you going to do with it? When it's finished, I mean?" Amy asked.

I had no idea.

I loved working on the circus, but I had never thought

about what would happen when it was finished. I think I had imagined we would go on building it forever.

Dad with Silvers Model Circus shortly before it went on display.

That evening, I asked Dad if he had any plans.

"Of course. It's going to go on exhibition."

"Really?"

I couldn't imagine how that would work.

"You don't think I would be doing all this without a plan, do you?" He laughed. "Once it's finished, we'll set it up somewhere so people can come to see it. We'll charge them something to come in, of course, and, if they like it, they will go home and tell all their friends about it."

It sounded so simple.

"How long do you think it will be before it's finished?" I asked.

"I've no idea. There's a long way to go yet, but I do know it will get done a lot quicker if you stop talking and do some work!"

Dad always expected me to pull my weight. He was an old-fashioned gentleman and believed that girls and women should be treated with respect, but he also believed they should be equals. In many ways, he was ahead of his time and taught David and me in exactly the same way.

His Australian heritage had given him a pioneer's approach to life, and he believed boys and girls both needed to learn as many practical skills as possible.

By the time I was sixteen, I could weld, strip down a car engine, use a saw efficiently and turn metal bearings on a lathe. David could bake, ice a cake, and even embroider, although I have never heard him admit it in public.

Career advice at Maynards was limited. There was a small room next to the school office which had a sign on the door saying CAREERS in large letters.

Inside, there was a table, two chairs and a shelf with a small collection of books and leaflets. The door was left unlocked each lunchtime, and we were told we could pop in whenever we liked.

I may have been the only pupil who visited the Careers Room as I spent many lunchtimes reading library books there and I don't remember ever being disturbed.

I looked through the leaflets once, but there was nothing that appealed to me. The books were more interesting and I remember that one of them had a section on drama schools. When I first found it, I was elated. I couldn't imagine why I hadn't thought of it before. If I wanted to act, then clearly, I should go to a drama school.

I read the chapter eagerly, and at the end, there was a list of contact details with the advice to approach each school directly and ask about their admission policies. I copied out the entire list and wrote to all of them.

I still hadn't told anyone about my ambition to be an actress, so I got up early each day for the next couple of weeks and hovered near the front door to intercept the post.

As I read through the replies, my heart sank. The schools all had similar selection processes and every single one of them included a singing audition.

I tore each letter into tiny pieces and flushed them down the toilet.

Although we received little advice about careers at Maynards, we were often asked which university we planned to attend. In those days, going to university was a rare achievement, but at Maynards it was expected that every girl would study for a degree. When I first told my teachers I didn't want to go to university, my decision was met with bewilderment and then veiled hostility. It was clear they felt I was squandering a great opportunity.

When my form tutor asked me what I intended to do with my life if I did not to go to university, I simply shrugged. I didn't know how to explain that I intended to travel around the country exhibiting a miniature circus.

Until then, I had been a model pupil, achieving high grades in all my subjects and never getting into trouble of any sort. I had worked hard to please my teachers and now I had a feeling I was letting them down.

I was still mourning my lost dream of becoming an actress, and as the other girls focused on which A-level grades they needed to get into their preferred university, I questioned why I was studying at all. For the first time in my life, I lost interest in schoolwork.

My grades dropped and my weight dropped too. My mother worried I had discovered boys and was secretly dieting, but the truth is I had no interest in anything. The only time I felt really happy was when I was at home working on the circus.

Mum became obsessed with feeding me. She had always insisted I eat something for breakfast, but now I refused. She offered me cereals, toast, or bacon and eggs. She even tried to tempt me with cake and biscuits, but the thought of eating made me feel sick. I didn't want to upset her, but I was finding it increasingly difficult to face food at all.

One morning, Mum insisted on weighing me and I can

remember her letting out a little gasp when she read the scales. I didn't feel thin, and I really didn't care whether I was thin or not, but I felt bad that I was worrying Mum. She asked if there was anything I would eat, and for some reason, I said rhubarb crumble.

After that, she got up early every morning and made me rhubarb crumble. I didn't want to eat it, but I felt too guilty to refuse.

Mum was watching me eat one morning when I finally admitted that I wanted to be an actress. She couldn't have looked more surprised if I had told her I wanted to clean drains.

"But it doesn't matter," I said quickly. "Because I can't sing."

"What do you mean, you can't sing?"

"There's something wrong with me. I can't do it."

I had never mentioned my visits to Mrs Mead, but now it all came tumbling out. Mum listened in silence, then put an arm around my shoulders.

"Listen, love, if you really want something in life, you can't just give up."

~

A few days later, Mum told me she had arranged for me to visit a neighbour called Mrs Graham. She was a vicar's wife and gave singing lessons.

My heart sank.

I knew Mum meant well, but she clearly hadn't understood what I had said. I couldn't sing. It was a fact. I didn't need to prove it again.

"No. I'm sorry, but I'm not going. It was embarrassing enough with Mrs Mead. I'm not going to make an idiot of myself again. Not in front of some vicar's wife."

"What difference does it make if she's a vicar's wife?" Mum frowned.

"I don't know. They all wear tweed skirts, don't they? And organise fetes and stuff."

"Don't be ridiculous. She's a lovely lady. And anyway, what have you got to lose?"

Before I rang Mrs Graham's doorbell, I peeked through her front window and groaned inwardly. The room was immaculate, with ornate pieces of china on every flat surface and religious paintings decorating the walls. What was I doing here?

I wanted to run, but instead, I pressed the doorbell and a dramatic blast of Rachmaninov rang out. It was so unexpected I burst into giggles.

A moment later, the door was opened by a small, round woman wearing a sensible tweed skirt, a pink jumper and a pearl necklace. She had a kind face and a broad smile.

"Come in, my dear, come in. You must be Diana."

She ushered me through to a small room dominated by an enormous, highly polished grand piano.

"Your mother tells me you can't sing. Is that right?"

I nodded.

"Well, let's see what we can do about that."

She settled herself on the piano stool and waved at an ancient leather armchair.

"Make yourself comfortable."

I sat down nervously and she continued, "First, tell me why you think you can't sing."

I explained what had happened at Maynards, and Mrs Graham nodded attentively.

When I finished, she turned to face the piano.

"Thank you for sharing that with me."

Her fingers ran lightly over the keys and a ripple of music filled the room.

"Stand up, please."

I rose obediently to my feet.

"Now, take a deep breath."

As I gulped air into my lungs, she played a single note and a familiar fear tensed my stomach.

"Can you sing that, dear?"

I opened my mouth and a strangled whine escaped.

"Just as I thought."

Closing the lid of the piano, Mrs Graham turned and smiled at me.

"We have a lot of work to do, don't we?"

Over the following months, I visited Mrs Graham every week, and, she taught me how to breathe, how to relax, and finally, how to use my breath to carry my voice out of my body.

She was kind and patient and showed me exactly how she herself used her breath to power her own magnificent voice.

She seemed convinced that I really could sing and slowly, because she believed in me, I began to believe in her. Instead of asking me to match my voice to the piano, she would sing a note herself and hold it while I wavered my voice up and down until, finally, I heard a matching harmony. It was a slow, difficult process, but my ear gradually learned to recognise tones and intervals.

As my confidence increased, I progressed to singing scales, arpeggios, and finally, songs.

At the end of each lesson, while she tidied up her music books, Mrs Graham told me little snippets about her life. I was surprised to discover she had not always been a vicar's wife.

She had been born into a musical family, and even as a small child, her voice had attracted a lot of attention.

I listened in amazement as she told me she had trained as an opera singer and had performed many leading roles on the London stage. Clearly, she adored the theatre and had relished her time in the spotlight.

One day, I asked her why she had given up her career.

"Love," she said simply. "I met Tom and everything changed. A vicar needs a wife to support him. We're a team, you see, Tom and me. It would never have worked if I'd still been on the stage."

"But don't you miss it? The theatre, I mean?"

"Of course, I do, my dear, every single day, but that's the thing about love, isn't it? It never comes without a cost."

I hadn't really thought about love before that.

Many of the girls in my class had boyfriends, but I had no idea how they managed to find them. The only males I met were David's friends and as I was sixteen and they were all in their mid-twenties, they felt like another generation.

In any case, I knew my mother would not approve. She often told me that girls shouldn't even think about getting married until they reached their thirties. She had been thirty-two before she met Dad.

And sometimes, she would add that if girls were not thinking about getting married, they had better keep away from men altogether.

Maynards was a male-free environment, but once we reached the sixth form, we could take part in two extra-curricular subjects each week which were organised jointly with Exeter School for Boys.

The novelty of sharing a classroom with the opposite sex caused a great deal of excitement. A huge amount of time and energy was spent discussing each boy and deciding who was the most fanciable. Amy considered herself above such conversations and told everyone she didn't intend to date until she was at least twenty-five and had achieved a first-class honours degree, but Jess and I surveyed our new classmates with interest.

I was still the quiet one of the class and I had a depressing feeling it was going to be as difficult finding a boyfriend as it had been to make friends with girls.

It came as a shock when, after the second lesson, a tall, angular youth caught up with me as we walked away from school.

"Did you know there's a fair in town this weekend?" he asked.

"No. Why?"

"I thought you might like to go."

I couldn't believe what was happening. A boy was asking me for a date. Or was he? He hadn't actually asked me to go with him.

"Maybe…" I replied uncertainly. "Are you going?"

"Yeah, I go every year."

"Oh."

There was an awkward silence.

"So, do you want to go, then?"

He really was asking me out.

"I can pick you up if you like," he offered, but I shook my head.

"No, I'll meet you at the entrance. Is seven-thirty okay?"

"Sure. See you then."

With a quick wave, he crossed the road and vanished around a corner.

I couldn't believe it. A boy had asked me out. I wanted to punch the air with excitement, but I was afraid people would stare at me.

It was only later that I realised I didn't know his name.

~

I knew Mum would never agree to me going to the fairground to meet a boy I hardly knew, so I spent the next two days persuading Amy and Jess to go with me.

Eventually, they agreed, and on Saturday evening, just before seven o'clock, I heard them knock on the front door as arranged. I was a little taken aback to find they were both wearing trousers suits and startling blue eye shadow in the style of ABBA.

Mum let me out of the house on the strict understanding I would be back before ten o'clock.

Jess and Amy teased me mercilessly all the way to the fairground. They found it hilarious that I didn't know my date's name and pointed to every boy we passed asking if it was him.

I didn't mind their teasing, but I was petrified I would be stood up. I kept thinking how excruciating it would be if we had to stand at the fairground entrance waiting for someone who never arrived. My stomach trembled at the thought.

I needn't have worried. He was standing at the entrance laughing with a group of other boys.

I had planned to act cool when I saw him, but I was so relieved he had turned up, I hurried straight over.

"I forgot to ask your name," I blurted out. "I'm Diana, by the way."

"I know, I'm Robin."

I winced as Amy and Jess dissolved into giggles. Why did he have to be called Robin? Why not Russel? Or Kurt? Mothers can be so cruel.

Robin's friends were looking at me and suddenly I felt self-conscious. Glancing down at my usual denim jeans and baggy T-shirt, I wished I had made more effort.

I noticed Robin was wearing a patterned shirt and fashionably flared trousers. He had an expensive-looking watch on his wrist and I realised my hands were still grimed with engine oil from helping Dad change his spark plugs that afternoon.

"Do you like Waltzers?" Robin asked.

I nodded. He had blue eyes and unruly blonde hair that reminded me of Bo from The Dukes of Hazzard.

I took out my purse at the pay desk, but Robin waved it away.

"Don't be daft," he grinned.

I had been on a Waltzer before, but never with a boy. Suddenly, everything was different.

The ride consisted of low cars, big enough for two or three people, that went around on a huge wooden carousel. The cars were like curved sofas with a steel bar across the front to hold the riders in place, and each one spun around in a circle, as well as lurching up and down, as the floor of the carousel rose and fell.

The result was a stomach-churning ride that drew squeals, groans, and gasps from the riders.

Robin slipped his arm around me, and as every jolt and twist of the car threw us together, I felt alive in a way I had never known. The Waltzer ran faster and faster until we were screaming in unison and the world around us dissolved into a whirling blur of colour.

By the time the car slowed to a stop, I was dizzy and laughing. I had never had so much fun in my life. Robin seemed to have an unlimited supply of cash, and we worked our way around every ride on the ground.

Finally, protesting that his stomach was too queasy to cope with any more, Robin suggested we try our luck on the side stalls.

I spotted Amy and Jess eating hotdogs with a group of boys from Exeter School and they waved us over to join them. Robin's queasiness didn't stop him from munching his way through an enormous bratwurst topped with onions and mustard.

I was finishing my hotdog when I spotted a shooting range. The outside was draped with plastic bags filled with marshmallows and humbugs and inside, on an elaborate stand, stood the largest box of chocolates I had ever seen.

"Wow!" I drooled. "That looks amazing!"

Robin grinned.

"You're a chocoholic? Me too!"

The stallholder assured us that all we needed to do to win the mighty box of chocolates was to shoot through the strings holding a row of plastic ducks in the air behind him.

He took Robin's money, handed him a battered air rifle, and placed six pellets on the counter in front of him.

"Take your time, mate. All you have to do is break the six strings."

"Go on, Robin, you can do it!"

Amy, Jess and the Exeter School boys came over to watch.

Robin took aim, and a duck bobbed sideways as the pellet brushed past its string.

"Never mind, mate," the stallholder cried encouragingly. "No chocolates, but you can still win one of the other prizes. Everyone's a winner!"

Robin reloaded and tried again. Another duck swung on its string and Amy giggled.

Four shots later, all the ducks were still swinging obstinately.

Robin grinned at me again and I noticed the cute way his eyes crinkled when he smiled.

"Do you really like chocolate?" he asked.

"I do."

"Then we're not leaving without that box," he announced and pulled more coins from his pocket.

He aimed the gun confidently, and I watched him fire again and again.

"Try aiming higher," I suggested. "You need to hit the string at the top where it's against the bar."

Robin kept firing, but the ducks kept bobbing on their strings.

"Give up, Rob. You're crap!" jeered a ginger-haired boy behind us.

"It's probably rigged," Amy said loudly. "I'll bet there's a wire in the string or something."

"I'm sure I hit that last one," Robin muttered.

"You're not supposed to hit the duck, you idiot!" the boy taunted.

"Piss off, Simon!" Robin snapped.

"Try aiming higher," I repeated. "You'll never break the string unless you hit it against the bar."

"Really?" Robin snapped. "You're an expert, are you?"

"It's obvious." I couldn't understand why he wouldn't listen to me.

"You're wasting your money," the ginger-haired boy gloated. "You could've bought the chocolates by now. They're probably out of date, anyway."

Robin slapped more coins on the counter, glared at the stallholder as he counted out the pellets, then took aim.

I watched silently until he fired the last pellet, then pulled some coins out of my purse.

"Six, please," I said to the stallholder.

I could feel Robin's eyes fix on me, and the group behind us suddenly went quiet.

Taking the gun, I loaded it, put it to my shoulder and lined up the sights. There was a crack and a soft thud as the pellet hit the top of the string, carrying it back against the metal bar. A moment later, the plastic duck floated gracefully to the ground.

Amy and Jess screeched with delight.

Buoyed by my success, I loaded another pellet, fired again, and another duck hit the ground.

"Go girl!" One of the boys clapped me on the shoulder and I felt a surge of pride. For once, I was the centre of attention and I was loving it.

I kept reloading and firing until all six ducks were on the

ground. Reluctantly, the stallholder lifted down the box of chocolates and handed it to me.

"Which is your favourite?" I asked Robin as I tore open the box, but he didn't answer. In fact, he hardly spoke for the rest of the evening.

I arrived home on the dot of ten and disappeared straight up to my bedroom. I couldn't believe that life could be so good. It had been a wonderful evening, and I finally had a real boyfriend of my own.

Robin had promised to phone me and I lay in bed happily, planning where we could go for our next date.

The next evening, I waited by the phone.

It took a full week before I realised Robin was never going to ring.

Mum insisted on visiting Granny every day. Since her trip to Australia, she seemed to have shrunk, and as winter set in, she developed bronchitis and her doctor suggested she go into hospital for some tests.

I knew Granny hated hospitals, but I reassured Mum that everything would be okay and went with her when she visited.

Mum had taken Granny into the hospital the previous day, while I was at school, but when we arrived at the bed Granny had been in, we found it empty.

At first, Mum guessed Granny had been moved to another ward, but when we asked a nurse, we could tell from her expression that something more serious had happened. We were ushered to a side room and, a few minutes later, a sister arrived to speak to us.

"I'm afraid there was an incident," she told us. "We should have been warned about your mother's condition."

"What do you mean? It was all in her notes, the bronchitis and the..."

"I am not referring to the bronchitis. I mean her mental condition."

The sister's tone was stern, and she frowned at us as she continued.

"If we had been warned in advance, alternative arrangements would have been made."

"I don't understand. What are you saying?" Mum's voice was trembling.

"My staff cannot be expected to cope with behaviour of that kind. They are here to provide a service to patients, not to be abused..."

"But what's happened?" I interrupted her. "What did she do?"

"She attacked a nurse who was trying to take a blood sample. Your grandmother bit her arm and hit her on the side of the head with a metal bowl."

I smiled despite myself.

"This is not a laughing matter!" the sister scolded. "The nurse had to have several stitches. It was also very upsetting for the other patients in the ward. Your grandmother was extremely abusive towards them and, in the end, two of our orderlies were forced to sedate her."

Mum gasped.

"Where is she? I have to see her."

"I'm sorry, but we couldn't keep her here. In the circumstances, it was decided to transfer her to Exminster."

"No! Don't send her there!" Mum was distraught. "It's an asylum! You can't move her to an asylum!"

The sister's tone was final.

"I'm sorry. It's too late. She's already there."

I had no idea what to expect as we made our way to Exminster Hospital.

To me, an asylum sounded like something from the Middle Ages. I had a vision of a dark gothic building tucked away in a back street, with studded wooden doors, low ceilings and iron bars on the windows.

It came as a surprise to find the hospital was outside the city, surrounded by open fields, and was approached by a long, tree-lined drive through an impressive entrance flanked by gatehouses.

The building itself was enormous. Three stories of solid red brick, punctuated by endless lines of white-framed windows, stretched in each direction. The architecture was classical and the two symmetrical wings, balancing the bulk of the main building, gave the feeling of a stately home rather than a municipal building.

As we stepped into the well-lit entrance hall, I was surprised to find an enormous chandelier sparkling above us. I began to think this might be a pleasant place to spend a few days, after all.

It was only when we approached a desk and Mum spoke to a nurse in an immaculate white uniform that my impression changed.

"Have you booked your visit?" the nurse asked curtly.

"Yes," Mum assured her. "I was told to be here at four-thirty."

"Then you're ten minutes early. Wait over there, please." Her gesture indicated a row of straight-backed chairs against the wall and we crossed to them obediently.

We sat in silence as a large grandfather clock ticked away the seconds and the nurse busied herself writing at the desk.

Every sixty seconds there was a gentle clunk as the minute hand worked its way around the clock face, until, with a subdued whirring noise, the timepiece sounded the half-hour and the nurse beckoned to us.

"This way, please."

We followed her along bright, sunlit corridors that looked out onto gravel forecourts, then up a staircase and through a warren of smaller corridors until she stopped in front of a locked door.

"She's in here," she said, turning a key. "Knock when you want to come out, but no more than thirty minutes."

Mum hesitated. "I was hoping to talk to her doctor."

"The doctor is not available at present," the nurse said quickly, "but I believe Mrs Spear is doing as well as can be expected."

As she ushered us through the door and locked it behind us, I had a sinking feeling in the pit of my stomach.

Ahead of us, a long room was empty apart from a few chairs and tables. The floor was bare wooden boards and the walls were plain white expanses without a picture of any description.

A row of doors opened to small rooms on one side, and as we walked past, I caught sight of iron bedsteads.

Ten or twelve patients were scattered around the main room. Some stared at us, but most were lost in their own worlds. One or two sat dejectedly on the floor, staring into space.

By a window, two elderly men waved their hands at each other and shouted words I couldn't understand. For a moment, I thought they were fighting, but then I realised they were not reacting to each other at all, but were simply repeating the same sounds and actions over and over again.

"Can you see her?" Mum asked.

I shook my head. "Maybe she's further down."

I looked around for a nurse but couldn't see one anywhere.

Suddenly, a stout, middle-aged woman in a floral dress grabbed me by the arm.

"Where is she?" she demanded. "I want my sister."

"I'm sorry..." I mumbled.

"She's not dead. I know she's not dead. I want my sister."

The woman reached up and stroked my hair. I pulled away but she had a firm grip on my arm.

"Do you know a lady called Hilda Spear?" Mum asked, but the woman didn't seem to hear. Her face was so close to mine I could feel her breath on my cheek.

"She's not dead, you know," she whispered.

Behind her, a tall skeleton of a man was unbuttoning his pyjamas. He dropped the shirt onto the floorboards with a dramatic flourish, then began to wriggle the trousers down over his bony hips.

I wanted to run to the door and beg the nurse to let me out, but I knew I couldn't abandon Mum.

With a great effort, I stayed calm. Lifting the woman's fingers from my hair, I gently pushed her away and looked around the room.

"There," I said, pointing to a figure crouched on a chair.

If I had not been looking for Granny, I would never have recognised her. She seemed tiny, dressed in a grey, wrap-around tunic that resembled a straightjacket. Her hair was uncombed and her face was pale without her customary mascara and red lipstick.

"Oh, my God!" Mum rushed over and threw her arms around Granny's thin shoulders. "Are you all right?"

Granny looked up with a pitiful expression.

"They think I'm mad," she said flatly. "They've sent me here to die."

Mum blinked back her tears. "Everything's going to be fine, I promise."

But Granny shook her head.

"No, it's not. They're going to kill me."

We tried to comfort her, but nothing we said made any difference. I could see she was terrified of the other patients. She flinched every time one came near, crossing her arms tightly across her chest and rocking herself backwards and forwards.

"You won't be here for long," Mum assured her. "I'm going to get you out. I promise."

~

It was almost a month before Granny was released. Mum visited her every day and I went with her on the weekends. Each time I saw her, I was shocked by how much Granny had aged. It was as if she was withering away before my eyes.

Every evening, Mum gave me a progress report. She had taken to phoning Granny's doctor daily and demanding to know why she had not yet been released. Each time she managed to speak to him, she was told more tests were needed.

Once when I visited, Granny had a series of dark bruises across her arms, but she couldn't tell us what had caused them. On another visit, she seemed to be heavily sedated and could hardly recognise us.

Finally, Mum insisted on seeing Granny's doctor herself, but she still couldn't get any clear answers about what was happening. She may have been Granny's next of kin, but Mum didn't seem to have any rights when it came to making decisions about Granny's treatment.

When a nurse admitted Granny was being tested for schizophrenia, Mum became very agitated.

"There's nothing wrong with her," she insisted. "I know she can be difficult, but she's not mad. You have to let her out."

I was surprised by Mum's outburst, but in the car on the way home, she told me that one of Granny's sisters had been diagnosed with schizophrenia in Australia and had been locked away in an asylum until she died.

One day, when I returned home from school, Mum was smiling.

"Good news! They're letting Granny out tomorrow."

"Great." I tried to sound enthusiastic. "What did the tests say?"

"I was right all along. There's nothing wrong with her. The doctors said that she just has 'uncontrollable anger', whatever that means."

"It means she's a vicious old bitch," David said bitterly.

"No, it doesn't." Mum glared at him. "It means that she can't help being the way she is."

"But is she really going to be all right looking after herself?"

"She'll be fine. I'll just have to keep an eye on her."

While Granny had been in Exminster, Mum had spent more time than ever working on the circus. I think, like the rest of us, she found it therapeutic to escape to a miniature world that was entirely separate from reality.

Every figure we created had its own personality, and we started to name them after our neighbours or characters from TV shows.

When gearwheels were needed to make new mechanisms, David and I donated our old toys, and one day I came home from school to find Dad had taken my toothbrush, which happened to be white, and had carved it to make tusks for an elephant.

We all made sacrifices for the circus, but it was undoubtedly Mum who made the most. Apart from giving up her dining room, she also let Dad cut up her brass curtain rods, "borrow" her food mixer to make papier mâché, and raid her jewellery box for gems to make sparkling eyes for the tigers.

She even let him fill her airing cupboard with wet chicken feathers that had been dyed bright colours to make plumes for the horses. The smell was indescribable.

I think even Mum was shocked, however, when she arrived home from shopping one day to find a large hole in the front door.

I was with Dad in his workshop when she burst in.

"Whatever's happened to the door?" she demanded.

"Ah, yes." Dad had the grace to look sheepish. "You don't mind, do you? The wood has such a lovely grain. I've been searching everywhere for something to carve the roof of the gold carriage..."

"Of course." Mum sighed resignedly. "I should have known."

Without another word, she turned and headed back to the house.

Dad grinned happily.

"I knew she'd understand."

Being dumped by Robin had been a traumatic experience, and I fully expected that I would never find another boyfriend, but, to my surprise, other boys did ask me out.

I decided it was easiest to say no straight away.

After watching my classmates, I had realised that having a boyfriend was not as exciting as I had thought it would be. When I spent time with David and his friends, they treated me as a younger sister and expected me to join in with whatever they were doing, whether that was working on a car, shooting clay pigeons or discussing the latest TV show.

But I now realised that girls and girlfriends are two very different things. As far as I could see, girlfriends had to wear dresses and makeup at all times and weren't expected to do anything except watch their boyfriends showing off. That was not a role that appealed to me.

I was perfectly happy on my own, but as the months went by, Jess and Amy became increasingly concerned that I didn't have a boyfriend. They each had a constantly changing group of admirers, and I often found it difficult to remember who was currently in favour.

I made the excuse that my mother didn't approve of me going out with boys, but Jess laughed at me.

"You're seventeen, for Christ's sake. A few months and you'll be an adult. You can do whatever you like."

"There's a new disco opening on Saturday," Amy added. "We'll pick you up. Your Mum won't mind if you're going with us."

It was hard to argue with them.

After that, the three of us spent every Saturday night at a disco. I often took a pair of earplugs that David used for shooting. The loud music didn't bother me so much when I was wearing them, but they made conversation impossible. Perhaps that was why, despite Jess and Amy's best efforts, I never found a boyfriend.

Mum tried to hide her disapproval of my new social life, but she couldn't quite manage it. I was always home a few minutes before the agreed time and she would always be sitting, waiting for me, with a suspicious expression on her face.

Dad's concerns were more practical. He knew my friends and I were mixing with boys from Exeter School and he also knew that many of them came from wealthy families. Some had been given sports cars as soon as they passed their driving tests, and several had already been involved in accidents. Drunk driving was a big problem with young drivers in the seventies and he was worried about me accepting lifts.

One evening, Dad called me downstairs and told me needed to talk to me. He sounded serious, and I was worried I must have done something wrong.

"Your mother and I have made a decision," he announced. "We don't like you having to rely on getting lifts from people when you go out, so we have decided to buy you a car."

I couldn't believe it. I knew things had not been going well at the printing factory and money was tight.

"You don't need to do that. I can always get a bus..."

"Come and look," Mum said.

I followed them outside and saw a white Vauxhall Viva parked by the kerb. The paintwork was dull and there were rust patches on the doors. One of the wing mirrors was missing and there was a chip on the front windscreen.

It was love at first sight.

"I'm going to call her Snowflake!" I announced, then grabbed Mum and Dad and hugged them tight. I knew, without a doubt, they were the best parents in the world.

CHAPTER 4

My first serious boyfriend was called Alister. He was a couple of years older than me but was still in the sixth form at Exeter School, as he had failed his A-levels and had returned to re-sit them. He was tall, thin and serious, with a mop of silky blonde hair that flopped across his eyes.

Alister's only ambition in life was to be a dentist. I never understood why. I didn't like the idea of any job that involved talking to people, but he genuinely wanted to wear a white coat and look at teeth.

Alister was nearly as quiet as me, and while the rest of the sixth formers were gyrating to ear-splitting glam rock in the school disco, the two of us would sit outside in the carpark watching the moon and planning the future.

I felt relaxed enough to be honest with Alister, but he didn't seem to notice. He often asked me what I wanted to do with my life, but when I told him I wanted to be an actress and travel the country with a model circus, he would laugh, gaze into my eyes and say, "But seriously, what do you really want to do?"

Coming home from school one afternoon, I found Mum sitting at the kitchen table while Dad poured her a cup of tea.

"What's wrong?" I asked.

"Nothing to worry about," Mum said brightly, but I didn't believe her.

"It's Granny," Dad said. "Mum arranged for a lady to help her clean her flat, but it didn't go well."

Mum sighed.

"It's my fault. I should have been there."

"No, it's not. That was the whole point. She needs a helper, so you don't have to keep going over there all the whole time."

"What happened?" I asked.

"Nothing much." Mum tried to smile. "No blood spilt."

"We can't go on like this, love." Dad's voice was quiet but firm. "You're making yourself ill. If she won't accept help from anyone but you, she's going to have to go into a home."

Mum sighed again.

"That's easy to say, but you know as well as I do that she'll never agree."

I didn't tell Alister about my singing lessons. And I hadn't told anyone at school about them either. I was sure they all remembered the day Mrs Mead embarrassed me in front of the whole class. The humiliation of that day still burned inside me and I had been careful never to risk repeating it. Every morning during school assembly, I dropped my head so my hair covered my face while I listened to the girls around me singing hymns.

For a while, I had even stopped going to birthday parties

because I was afraid of having to sing "Happy Birthday to You".

But now, after a year of practising, Mrs Graham had told me I was ready to sing in public. I resisted at first, but she reminded me that if I really wanted to audition for drama school, I would have to face my fears.

Nearly half the girls at Maynards sang in the school choir. To me, it felt like a secret society that I would never be allowed to join. At the beginning of each year, girls who wanted to be in the choir were told to report to Mrs Mead in the music room, but the thought of asking her to give me another chance was more than I could face.

I took the coward's way out and crept into a choir rehearsal when no one was looking. There was a pile of spare song sheets on a table by the door, so I took one and stood awkwardly on the end of a row, feeling like a beggar at a banquet.

I was sure Mrs Mead would recognise me, but she was busy sorting out her music. Finally, she sat down at the piano, barked instructions over her shoulder, and began to play.

The choir sang, and after a moment of panic, I joined in. I whispered at first, but I could tell my voice was in harmony and gradually my confidence rose.

Soon I was enjoying myself. I couldn't believe it. No one had laughed. No one had tried to stop me. I felt as if I could fly. As we filed out of the hall at the end of the rehearsal, I caught Mrs Mead's eye. A cold sweat broke out down my spine because I knew she was going to confront me, demand an explanation, but to my amazement, she merely smiled and looked away.

I was stunned. Mrs Mead didn't remember me. She had inflicted a wound that would stay with me for the rest of my life and she didn't even remember.

From then on, I was a regular member of the choir. We

rehearsed every Monday and Wednesday and sang in school competitions and church halls. I took the song sheets home so that Mrs Graham could help me practise and my confidence blossomed.

~

As our A-level exams approached, everyone at school began to panic. Most of the girls had offers from universities that depended on them achieving a particular grade, and every conversation in the form room revolved around boys or grades. As I was happy with Alister and wasn't worried about my grades, I felt more of an outsider than ever.

Alister was also taking physics and math, so we often revised together, but I didn't enjoy it much as Alister took studying so seriously. He had already taken his A-levels twice, and he knew this was his last chance to achieve his dream. I felt sorry for him.

I hoped that, once the exams were over, he would relax, but instead he became increasingly stressed. And it wasn't only Alister. Jess and Amy became emotional wrecks, and many of our classmates struggled to cope with the long summer wait for their results.

Fortunately, drugs were not easily available in Exeter in the late seventies, and although there was always someone who had a friend who could supply, most teenagers treated "wacky backy" and unidentified tablets with suspicion.

Alcohol, however, was socially acceptable. Now that we had all turned eighteen, passing out in nightclubs, throwing up in bushes or even waking up with no recollection of the previous evening seemed to be accepted as a normal part of growing up.

At least that was how it seemed to be for my classmates.

In my house, things were different. Mum had been brought up in poverty in the East End of London and she detested anything that reminded her of those days. Neither she nor my father drank, and she had no tolerance for anything that she considered to be coarse behaviour.

As a result, I went to great lengths not to be seen doing anything that would upset her.

~

As soon as I left Maynards, I started full time at the printing factory. It was hard work, but I enjoyed being with my family and I knew I would only be there until we finished the circus.

I felt I would be letting everyone down if I left home before the circus was finished, but once it was on exhibition, I would be free to apply to drama school.

In my mind, I had everything planned, but I hadn't yet worked out how I was going to break the news to my parents. We were a tightly bound family unit, and I wasn't sure how they would react. Dad's illness and Mum's problems with Granny meant David and I had always provided a lot of support and I didn't want them to feel I was abandoning them.

It was a nagging worry at the back of my mind, but with the optimism of inexperience, I convinced myself that everything would turn out fine.

~

Although Alister and I had been together for months, I still hadn't introduced him to my parents. He would have been most people's idea of a perfect son-in-law. He was polite, hardworking, well-dressed and intelligent, but I knew that would not be enough to impress my mother. Deep down, I knew no one was ever going to be good enough to impress my mother.

One morning, as summer reached its peak, an envelope

with the dreaded exam results landed on our doormat. I tore it open and discovered I had four good results. Mum and Dad were delighted.

I was about to call Alister when he rang me.

"What did you get?" I asked.

"Not enough," he said flatly. "I'm still one grade short."

Even over the phone, I could feel his pain.

"Do you want to meet up? We could go to the cinema or something?"

"No. I think I'd be better on my own for a bit."

I wanted to reach down the phone and hug him, but instead I heard myself say, "Okay, 'bye then."

The following day, Alister phoned back, and we walked into town and sat together on the Cathedral Green.

"So, what are you going to do?" I asked.

"A course in forensic science. It's in central London. Dad's been onto them and they've accepted my grades."

He looked miserable.

"But is that what you want?" I asked.

"Of course not!" he snapped. "All I've ever wanted is to be a dentist, but it's not going to happen, is it?"

"Surely there must still be a way?"

"I can't take my A-levels again."

"But if forensic science isn't what you want to do…" I persisted

"Grow up, Diana!" he erupted. "It's so easy for you, isn't it? I'd die for the grades you've got and you're not even going to use them! Sometimes, you make me sick!"

Heads turned in our direction.

"I was only trying to help…" I protested.

"Don't bother. My life is shit and there's nothing you can do about it."

I knew it wasn't me that had made him angry, but as he stood up and walked away, I couldn't stop myself feeling guilty.

A few weeks later, when Alister left for London, he promised to stay in touch. As we waited for his train at the station, he told me he would come back to visit as soon as he could, but we both knew he would not.

By the end of September, Mum was visiting Granny twice a day in between working at the printing factory and she looked exhausted.

One Saturday, I went with her and was surprised to find Granny still in bed when we arrived at half past ten.

"Is she all right?" I asked.

"It's probably her tablets. The doctor warned they might make her sleepy."

Mum woke Granny and we helped her to get dressed.

The old lady seemed confused and, by the time Mum had settled her at the kitchen table, she was in a foul temper.

"Where's my breakfast?"

"It's just coming," I assured her as Mum shovelled bacon and eggs on to a plate.

"It's not right, letting an old woman go hungry," Granny muttered.

Suddenly, she snatched a fork and smashed it down on the table, driving the metal tines deep into the wood inches from my fingers.

"You nearly stabbed me!" I wailed.

"Shouldn't keep me waiting then," Granny snarled.

Mum ignored the fork as she slid the plate onto the table. "There, you'll feel better, now."

As I drove home, Mum sat slumped in the passenger seat. Glancing at her, I noticed the tight lines around her lips and the heavy shadows under her eyes.

"You can't keep doing this," I said. "She doesn't deserve it."

"She's my mother."

"So? It doesn't make you her slave."

Mum blinked and wiped a hand across her eyes.

"You don't understand. She wasn't always like this. There were difficult times when I was little. Really difficult. And Mum worked day and night just to keep food on the table. I can't abandon her now."

"But you're wearing out."

"I'm fine."

"You're not, it's time..."

"No! I've told you. I'm fine. I don't want to hear any more about it."

Clearly, Mum was not in a mood to listen, but later, I talked to Dad and David.

"I'm really worried about her. She's making herself ill running around after Granny and it's only going to get worse."

"I know," Dad agreed. "I'm worried about her too, but I can't see an answer."

"Shoot the old witch?" David suggested. "Put us all out of our misery?"

I frowned at him.

"Seriously, we have to think of something."

The following evening, I was upstairs when I heard the phone ring. A few minutes later, David poked his head around my bedroom door. He looked worried.

"What is it?" I asked.

"It was the woman who lives next door to Granny. She says she's standing in the road in her nightie trying to stop the traffic."

"What?"

"Shall I tell Mum?" he asked.

"No, it's not fair. We need to deal with it."

Moments later, I was downstairs.

"David and I are popping over to see Granny," I said as calmly as I could. "Her neighbour rang to say she's being a bit odd."

"Nothing unusual there, then," Dad said.

"I'll come with you," Mum began, but I interrupted her.

"No, don't worry. We'll be fine."

We found Granny standing on the grass verge outside her flat. She was wearing a thin cotton nightie and her bare feet were muddy and wet.

"Is everything okay?" I asked carefully.

"Buggers won't stop."

Her hand flicked out in front of her and there was a clacking sound as something ricocheted off a passing car.

"Granny! You can't throw stones at the cars!"

"Buggers won't stop," she repeated irritably.

"But, why do you want them to stop?" David asked.

"Can't light the fire!" Granny spat out the words. "No matches. Just want matches, but the buggers won't stop."

"You're getting cold. Why don't we go back inside?"

I tried to take her arm, but Granny shook me off.

"Need matches," she growled.

"No, you don't need matches," David said firmly. "Your fire's electric, anyway."

"Matches!"

Granny shoved David away from her and shot another stone at the passing traffic.

"Don't worry, Granny," I said. "David will get some matches. You come inside with me."

David gave me a confused look, so I made a "play-along-with-me" face at him and ushered Granny back towards the flat.

The front door was wide open, and as we stepped into the living room, I saw the floor around the electric fire was littered with spent matches. Some had burned holes in the carpet and there were scorch marks on the skirting boards.

"You could've burned the place down!" I gasped. "Whatever were you thinking?"

"It's cold."

Granny's voice was still defiant, but now she sounded like a child.

Turning back to her, I saw she was shivering, and for the first time in my life, I felt sorry for her. She was confused and frightened.

I took off my coat, wrapped it around her, then cleared away the matches and turned on the fire.

"What are we going to do?" I asked David. "She's not safe on her own."

"I know."

His face was drawn as he considered Granny, who was curled up on the sofa, snoring softly.

"She needs to be in a home. Not an asylum, just somewhere people can look after her."

"She won't agree to it," I said flatly, "and I don't think a home would take her. You know what she's like."

"Well, she can't live with us. It would either end with me strangling her or Mum being sent to the asylum."

"That's not funny," I snapped.

"I wasn't joking," he snapped back.

"But what can we do? Things are only going to get worse."

"Maybe her doctor can help?"

"Good thinking. I'll phone the surgery in the morning. They'll be closed now, but what are we going to do until then? We can't just leave her here. God knows what she'll do."

"I don't think we've got any choice, have we?" he muttered. "We're going to have to stay here tonight."

I left David watching Granny and went home.

I'm sure Mum knew I was not being strictly accurate when I told her Granny wasn't feeling well and we didn't want to leave her alone, but she accepted my explanations and helped me pack a few things for the night.

I had expected her to insist on coming back to the flat with me, but I could see she was exhausted and was relieved David and I were prepared to take her place.

"If she asks for me, just phone and Dad will drop me over. Are you sure you'll be okay?"

"Of course." I tried to smile. "After all, it's only for one night."

Dad dropped me back to the flat, and on the way, I admitted I hadn't told Mum the whole truth of what had happened.

"You don't have to go back if you don't want to," Dad said. "I'll stay with David."

I was tempted to accept his offer, but I was worried he would slip into another headache and David would have two people to look after.

"No, it's fine," I assured him. "If she gets upset, I'll give her some more of her tablets. Mum says they're supposed to calm her down."

Dad nodded.

"Okay," he agreed, "but call me if you have any problems."

I found David alone watching TV.

"Where is she?" I asked.

"In the bedroom. When she woke up, she started asking for Trixie. I said I didn't know who Trixie was, but she kept insisting she'd been here earlier."

"She's got a sister called Trixie, hasn't she? Maybe she was dreaming about her."

"Maybe," David agreed. "Anyway, she just glared at me, like she does, then marched into the bedroom and slammed the door. I thought she'd be safe enough in there for the moment, so I left her to it."

"Okay. I suppose I'd better check on her."

Granny was sitting at her dressing table staring into the mirror.

"Hello, there. Are you all right?"

As she looked up, Granny saw my reflection in the mirror and a pathetic hope lit her face.

"Trixie!" She reached out a hand to me. "I knew you'd come back."

"It's me, Granny, it's Diana."

She squeezed my fingers, and I flinched as her nails bit into my flesh.

"You have to help me, Trixie. You have to..."

Suddenly, she stopped and her eyes flicked to the corner of the room.

"What's that?" she asked.

"What's what?"

"There." She pointed at the floor and her eyes opened wide with fear. "What's it doing?"

"I can't see anything."

"The trapdoor! It's moving!"

Her fear was infectious, and I felt the hairs on my arms rise.

"You're imagining it," I said, trying to get a grip on myself. "There is no trapdoor."

Her voice rose to a shriek.

"They're coming up! The little red men! Trixie! Stop them!"

I wasn't afraid of the little red men, but I had never been more terrified of my grandmother.

"It's okay." I stammered. "They won't hurt you…"

"Kill them!" she screamed. "Squash the little bastards!"

"Okay! Okay!"

To my surprise, I found myself stomping about on the threadbare carpet.

"Over there!" Granny cried, pointing at another invisible creature. "Get him!"

"I've got him!" I shouted back as I stamped hard on the floor.

"Quick! There's another one!"

I lashed out, kicking and stamping in every direction, until Granny flopped back against the dressing table.

"That's taught them," she gasped. "They won't be back for a while."

She was swaying dangerously on the stool, so I helped her to the bed and in minutes she was asleep.

When I returned to the lounge, David was still watching TV.

"What have you been up to?" he asked.

"Killing little red men," I answered irritably. "She's asleep for now, but it's going to be a long night."

~

Mum had sent a parcel of food over, so David and I found some plates and divided everything into three portions.

We left the lounge door open so that we would hear

Granny if she headed towards the front door and sat down to eat.

A heavy stillness permeated the flat, and I was filled with apprehension.

"Do you feel as though you're waiting for something to happen?" I asked David.

"Sort of," he agreed, "but I guess that's not surprising. Being around Granny always puts me on edge. Hopefully tomorrow we can get things sorted."

As the hours ticked by, we took it in turns to check on Granny, but she snored on undisturbed. I tried to wake her once, but she only grunted and turned over, so I gave up, deciding that if she was hungry, she would wake by herself.

After watching the late-night news, we found a pile of blankets in the airing cupboard and settled ourselves as best we could. David insisted I stretch out on the sofa while he tried to get comfortable on a white, faux-leather armchair.

"Stupid bloody thing," he muttered, "it's so damned slippery I keep sliding off."

He looked thoroughly miserable with his legs braced against the coffee table and a rose-pink blanket draped across him. Suddenly, the absurdity of the situation hit me and I began to giggle.

"I'm glad you think this is funny," David grumbled. "I'm going to be awake all night at this rate."

"Then try sleeping in the bath," I grinned.

"No way! I'm not risking waking up in the middle of the night with Granny sat on the loo next to me!"

I burst out laughing, and the tension inside me eased.

"That would give you nightmares," I agreed.

Despite our fears, we must have both fallen asleep quite quickly because I woke, with a start, shortly after midnight.

The television was screening an ancient cowboy film and David was slumped in the armchair.

I wondered what had woken me, and as I listened, I heard a scrabbling noise coming from Granny's bedroom. I thought about waking David, but he looked peaceful where he was, so I unwrapped my blanket and stood up.

I tapped on Granny's door, but when there was no answer, I pushed it open.

Granny was standing by her bed next to an open suitcase. She looked up as I came in and held a finger to her lips.

"Shh!"

"What are you doing?" I asked.

She didn't answer but pulled open the wardrobe door and began bundling clothes into the suitcase.

I knew if I tried to stop her, she would get angry, so I thought it best to humour her. Hopefully, she would soon get tired and go back to bed.

"That's a pretty dress," I said, trying to sound casual.

"You can't have it, Trixie," Granny snapped. "It's mine."

"I'm Diana, remember?"

"I'll be off soon."

"It's very late. Wouldn't it be better to wait until morning?"

"No!" She shook her head as if trying to clear her thoughts. "Have to go when I've done it."

"When you've done what?" I asked.

She looked at me as if I were an idiot.

"Got rid of the Catholic."

"What do you mean? There aren't any Catholics here…"

"Yes, there are. In there. On the chair. I've been watching him."

"That's David. He's your grandson..."

"Can't trust Catholics," she muttered. "They want to lock me away. Here, look."

Her bony fingers lifted the edge of the pillow, and I caught a flash of something beneath it.

"What's that?" I asked. "Can I see?"

Granny lifted the pillow a little higher, and I had a clear view of a large, heavy-bladed kitchen knife.

"That'll do the job!" she gloated.

Suddenly, my heart was pumping so hard I could barely breathe.

I had no idea what to do. Did she really mean to stab David? Every instinct told me she did.

I was taller than her, and stronger than her, but I was also petrified. Should I try to snatch the knife? Could I get it away from her or would we end up in a wrestling match?

The blade was long and gleaming. What if she turned it on me? There had to be another way.

"Are you hungry?" I asked, trying to keep my voice steady. "There's some chicken in the kitchen if you want it."

She was busy with the suitcase as I edged towards the door.

"Tell you what, you keep packing and I'll bring some in here. That's the best idea."

I backed out of the room, keeping my eyes on her as I went.

David grunted as I shook him awake.

"She's got a knife!" I hissed. "She wants to kill you!"

He struggled to sit up.

"Why? What have I done?"

"Nothing. She's off her head. She thinks you're a Catholic."

"You're joking?"

"No! She's got a knife. It's under her pillow in the bedroom."

"What do we do?" he asked, wide-eyed. "Call the police?"

"I don't know? Should we?"

"Maybe... I don't know? What do you think?"

"I don't know..."

We stood, gazing at the bedroom door, afraid Granny would come bursting through it.

"This is ridiculous," David said at last. "She's tiny. And there's two of us. We shouldn't be afraid of her."

"It's a bloody big knife," I reminded him.

"If she sees me, surely she'll know who I am?"

I wasn't convinced.

"She thinks I'm Trixie, remember? And she's been seeing little red men coming up through the floor. I wouldn't put any money on her being rational right now."

"It's gone very quiet. What do you think she's doing?"

"No idea."

We stood for a long time listening until, finally, we heard the sound of Granny snoring.

"Now what?" David asked.

"I don't know. I'll take a look."

"Be careful."

"Of course, I'll be bloody careful!"

Slowly, to avoid making the smallest noise, I turned the handle and pushed the bedroom door open. Inside, Granny was sprawled across the bed, her head on the open lid of the suitcase.

I tiptoed into the room. Granny's breathing was erratic, and every time she moved, I froze. Reaching the bed, I slid my fingers under the pillow and felt the smooth shape of the knife handle.

Trying not to breathe, I gripped the handle and pulled it out.

"Oh, my God!"

David flinched when I showed him the knife. "Do you think she's got anything else in there?"

"Possibly. Do you think we should look?"

"No. Let's not risk waking her up."

We spent the rest of the night perched on the sofa, staring at the bedroom door.

~

On the dot of eight in the morning I phoned the doctor's surgery. The receptionist told me they no longer did home visits but I was not in the mood to listen.

"It's an emergency!" I insisted. "My grandmother's very ill. We can't bring her to the surgery. We need a doctor here straight away!"

The doctor arrived in the afternoon.

Fortunately, Granny seemed to have forgotten about the knife and was sitting, staring out of her bedroom window, when the doorbell rang.

"I've been told there's an emergency," the said doctor said brusquely. "Where is she?"

"In her bedroom but..."

He pushed past me before I had a chance to say anything else.

"What seems to be the problem?" he asked Granny.

She turned, looked him up and down, then went back to staring out of the window.

"Is she eating?" the doctor asked.

"Like a horse," David was standing behind me in the doorway.

"Has she had any fever?"

"No," I replied.

"Any injuries or bleeding?"

"No."

"Blackouts?"

"I don't think so..."

"Then you need to bring her to the surgery. I'm afraid I have a very busy—"

"No!" I cut across him. "You have to help us!"

The doctor hesitated, and I signalled him to follow me into the hall.

"I can't talk in front of her," I explained, "but you have to listen."

I gave a brief account of what had happened during the night while the doctor stood tapping the toe of his shoe against his medical bag. When I finished, he shook his head dismissively.

"I'm afraid I can't help you," he said. "I'm only concerned with her physical wellbeing and she doesn't seem to have any conditions that are causing concern at present."

"What!" I couldn't believe what I was hearing. "She was trying to light an electric fire with matches. If she sets fire to the house won't that affect her physical wellbeing?"

"I appreciate these things are upsetting for you, but it's not uncommon in elderly patients..."

"She's not safe to be on her own," I insisted.

"Is there anyone she can stay with? Your parents, perhaps? Many families find themselves having to take in elderly relatives when they can't cope on their own."

"No!" I was surprised by the anger in my voice. "Granny is not moving in with us! My mother has looked after her all her life and now she's worn out. She can't do it anymore."

"Well, I'm sorry, but you'll have to try the social services..."

"No!" I was exhausted and reaching the end of my tether. "I'm asking you! Granny isn't like other old ladies. If she gets upset, she'll attack someone. She's not mad. She's just old and confused. She doesn't need to be in an asylum but she does need someone to look after her."

"I'm really sorry, but I'm afraid I can't help you." The doctor's voice was still firm but it was less patronising than before. "It's current thinking that patients with mental problems are better served in the community. A lot of the secure units and asylums are being closed down at the moment, which means it's almost impossible to find a place in a care home."

I had noticed David slip into the kitchen, now he appeared beside me and held out the carving knife.

The doctor flinched.

"She was planning to stab me with this last night," David said. "If we walk out and leave her alone, there's no way of telling what she will do next. She's your patient, so doesn't that mean that if she does stab someone, you'll be responsible?"

There was a long silence as the doctor considered.

"Very well," he said at last. "I'll make some calls but I'm not promising anything."

~

Mum wept with relief when I told her Granny had been moved into a residential home that provided care for people with dementia. It had locks on the doors and windows, but the staff were kind and friendly.

"Do they have visiting hours? I'll have to see if there's anything she needs."

"Don't worry. She's fine for now. You don't need to rush over there. David and I will keep visiting her. Why don't you wait until she asks for you? Then you can go to see her."

Mum gave me a strange look.

"All right," she agreed. "I won't go yet, but as soon as she asks for me, I'll go straight over."

Granny lived peacefully at the residential home for over four years but she never once mentioned Mum.

And Mum never saw her again.

CHAPTER 5

Mrs Graham was the only person I had told that I wanted to apply to drama school. I had been afraid she would try to talk me out of it but, instead, she encouraged me to prepare a few songs that I could sing unaccompanied at auditions.

"It might help if you can get some acting experience too," she suggested. "Were you in any plays at school?"

"No. They don't do drama at Maynards. I used to belong to Young Northcott but I had to leave."

"That's a shame. You really ought to have something to put down on your application. Aren't there any amateur dramatic clubs you could join?"

It was such an obvious suggestion I was surprised it had not occurred to me before.

"Some of my friends used to belong to the Exeter Little Theatre," Mrs Graham told me. "When they were younger, that is. It might be worth going along to one of their meetings."

That night I lay in bed and considered the suggestion. If I was serious about following my dreams, I knew I had to start working towards them. The thought of meeting new people was still daunting but I had a simple idea to make things easier. I would persuade David to go with me.

~

It was an icy Wednesday evening in the middle of January when I found myself standing outside the Little Theatre clubhouse.

From inside, I could hear people laughing and chatting. They sounded relaxed and happy and I immediately felt I had made a mistake. I didn't want to go in among all those strangers. I wanted to turn around and run, but David was beside me.

"We should have let someone know we were coming," I began. "Maybe we should come back another time."

"We're here now. We might as well go in," David said and pushed the door open.

I hesitated for a moment, then followed him inside.

I think I had been expecting something more formal, perhaps a receptionist on the door taking names, but I was faced with a room full of people who were all absorbed with their own conversations and I had no idea what to do.

David immediately started talking to a young man with shoulder-length black hair and a drooping moustache while I stood awkwardly, regretting my decision to come.

A burst of laughter erupted in a corner and I looked over to see a group gathered around a dark-haired man who was clearly telling a story. He had the most wonderfully expressive hands that floated in the air in front of him, his fingers outspread, illustrating everything he said. I wondered if he might be Italian. He finished with a dramatic flourish and another round of laughter broke out.

As the man looked up, he caught my eye and a friendly smile spread across his face.

Excusing himself, he strode across the room.

"New members?" he asked. "You're very welcome. My name is Robert, by the way, but everyone calls me Bob."

David and I introduced ourselves and Bob told us a little about the company.

"You've come at a good time. Now the pantomime's out of the way we're planning our productions for the next year. Have you had much experience on stage?"

David did not need any encouragement. He launched into a description of his exploits with Young Northcott and he and Bob were soon laughing like old friends.

"And what about you?"

There was a warmth in Bob's voice that made me feel he was genuinely interested, and to my surprise, I found myself telling him that I wanted to act.

"Perfect."

He smiled and picked up a script from a pile on a table nearby. "We have auditions for our March production next week. If there's a part that appeals to you, why not give it a go?"

As I took the script, a voice in my head was screaming at me to drop it and run for the door. Instead, I took a deep breath and looked straight into Bob's eyes.

"Great, I'll do that."

~

The play was a Victorian melodrama about Salvatore Ferraro, a heartless manservant who tricked an elderly heiress into marrying him then killed her for her fortune.

The main female parts were too old for me but there was a maid called Assunta who was seduced by Salvatore then abandoned by him. It was not a large part but it had several decent speeches and I desperately wanted it.

By the following Wednesday I had practised all of Assunta's lines so many times I knew every scene by heart.

David came with me to the auditions. I was disappointed to find that Bob was not there but David had already made friends with half the company, so, with butterflies in my stomach, I stood beside him, listening to him chatting until it was time for the auditions to begin.

There were several other girls trying for the part of Assunta, and it was obvious that most of them had been club members for some time. My name was the last on the list, and as I waited, I could see nods of approval and little gestures of encouragement as each girl stepped up to take her turn.

I guessed it would be a long time before a new member would be offered a part. The thought was strangely reassuring and once I realised I had little chance of succeeding, the butterflies in my stomach disappeared.

The following Wednesday, David and I arrived at the clubhouse to find rows of chairs standing in a semicircle. We settled ourselves at the back, and the room was soon packed.

I wondering whether Bob would turn up. There was something about his smile that had stayed in my mind.

An elderly man stepped up to the front of the room and clapped his hands.

"Okay, everyone. Let's have a bit of hush, shall we?"

There was a buzz of excitement as heads turned towards him.

"I think everyone knows me, but in case there are any new members here, my name is Henry and I'm the chairman. Mainly because no one else wants the job!"

There was a burst of applause and Henry bowed politely.

"Thank you so much. I'm sure you all want to know the result of the auditions last week, so let's get that out of the way first, shall we?"

He pulled a piece of paper from his pocket.

"Drum roll, please."

I jumped as the couple beside me stamped their feet on the floor.

"Okay," Henry grinned. "That'll do. No need to get overexcited."

With a flourish, he unfolded the paper.

"The part of Salvatore will be played by Robert Townsend."

There was another burst of applause, and heads turned towards the door. Looking around, I saw Bob had arrived and his smile was as dazzling as I remembered.

Henry continued reading from the list and enthusiastic clapping greeted each name.

"And the part of Assunta goes to Diana Hardie," Henry announced. "I believe Diana is a new member. Perhaps you'd like to stand up, Diana?"

As I rose to my feet, all eyes swivelled in my direction, and for once, I didn't feel embarrassed. Instead, I felt elated.

"Congratulations!" Bob beamed at me a few minutes later. "It's a great little play and we've got some of our best actors in the cast, so I'm sure you're going to enjoy yourself."

I grinned back happily. I knew he was right.

I arrived early for the first rehearsal and found Bob in the club room talking to a short, round man with an infectious laugh.

"Ahhh! This must be my Assunta!" the man trilled as he saw me.

"Hello Diana, this is Tom," Bob smiled. "He's our director. Don't worry, if you've heard any rumours about him, most of them aren't true."

I hadn't heard anything about Tom, and I wasn't sure what to say.

"Ignore him, dear girl. I can assure you everything you have heard is an understatement."

Tom waved a hand dramatically in my direction and I stepped back instinctively. My foot caught against a small table and sent it crashing. Looking behind me, I saw the splintered remains of one leg lying on the floor.

"I'm sorry," I gasped, "I didn't see that there."

"Another priceless antique bites the dust," Tom sighed.

"Don't worry, it's just an old prop," Bob said as he picked up the pieces and leaned them against the wall.

"I'm sorry," I repeated, "my grandmother says I was born with the clumsy gene."

Bob waved a hand dismissively.

"Forget it. A bit of glue and it will be fine."

"If you've finished demolishing my set, can we please get on with the rehearsal?" Tom sniffed as the door opened and the rest of the cast walked in.

Bob introduced me to Sara and Jenny, the two ladies playing the main roles, and whispered to me later that they had both been classically trained and had worked for many years in repertory theatre. Now they acted for their own pleasure, but it was clear they took the production very seriously and expected everyone else to reach their high standards.

I wasn't sure what to make of Tom. He was loud and demanding, but he was also patient and had a wicked sense of humour. He was forever making suggestive comments, and I had no idea what most of them meant.

I soon realised Sara and Jenny didn't approve of Tom. They glided through the rehearsals like swans on a lake while Tom was a small terrier yapping at them from the bank. He insisted on calling them the Old Spinsters, which he said referred to the parts they were playing, but I think he just liked to annoy them.

Bob spent a lot of time keeping the peace. He was very good at calming Sara and Jenny when Tom upset them, and without him, I'm sure the rehearsals would have descended into chaos.

"He really is an old devil," Bob grinned when Tom made yet another outrageous comment. "But he doesn't mean any harm."

"Well, I think it's most unprofessional," Sara sniffed haughtily. "I really think he should restrain himself."

~

As the rehearsals continued, I got to know the other club members and soon felt at home at the Little Theatre.

There was a group of about twenty core members, and David and I were welcomed by everyone. On club nights and after rehearsals, they met at the local pub and drank and laughed until closing time. After that, a smaller group would make their way back to someone's house and an informal party would carry on until the early hours of the morning.

Bob was nearly always there, and I found it easy to share my hopes and dreams with him.

As the weeks went by, we spent hours talking about every subject imaginable.

To my surprise, I found Bob listened to me, and although he laughed a lot, he never mocked my ideas. He grinned broadly when I told him I was encouraging snails into my garden to rebalance its wildlife, and in return, he told me stories of his childhood adventures on his uncle's pig farm.

Bob loved history as much as I did and we talked about the Mongols, the Spanish Conquistadors, ancient Chinese dynasties and the fact that schools rarely taught anything that happened outside Europe.

We didn't always agree, but we talked and laughed and I felt free to be myself. It was wonderful.

I had expected to be nervous as the dress rehearsal approached, but instead, I found myself cocooned in a happy bubble. Everything in my life was perfect. I enjoyed working with my family during the day and I loved rehearsing and spending time with Bob each evening.

I wished things could go on, just as they were, forever.

~

The dress rehearsal turned out to be utter chaos. Carpenters were still building the set and there was a ladder in the middle of the stage where an electrician was busy setting spotlights, but I didn't care. It all added to the excitement.

On Monday evening, when I arrived at the theatre ready for the first night, I was relieved to see the set was finished and looked excellent. Club members had loaned various pieces of furniture, and there was even a magnificent chaise longue in the middle of the stage.

I hurried to the dressing rooms and changed into my black maid's costume before having one last read through my lines.

Assunta had to walk onto the stage as soon as the curtain rose. The set would be lit by a warm red glow, as if the last rays of the setting sun were filtering through the window. Then, as the introductory music faded, I was to mime lighting an oil lamp while a technician brought up the main lights on stage. Everything had worked perfectly in the dress rehearsal, and I was eager to get started.

As this was 1979, there were no restrictions about having real flames on stage. I had been told to light a match, then turn upstage so my body would mask the flame from the audience as I held my hand towards the oil lamp and pretended to light the wick. As soon as the stage lights went on, I had to turn back to the audience and blow out the match.

When the five-minute call rang out, I was already at the side of the stage listening as the audience settled into their seats. I could hardly believe this was really happening.

The introductory music finished, the curtains rose, the stage manager gave me my cue, and I walked out across the stage.

Tiny beads of sweat ran down my back under the tight costume and every nerve in my body was taut with excitement. I held my head high and tried not to think about the hundreds of pairs of eyes that were watching me as, with a confident flourish, I struck the match and held it towards the oil lamp.

The flame gleamed brightly and I waited for the stage lights to go up.

Nothing.

I waited a little longer. I willed the light in the lamp to come on, but still nothing happened. I hesitated, swallowing hard, as the match burned closer and closer to my fingers.

At last, the stage lights blazed on and I breathed a sigh of relief.

I blew out the match and was about to walk off stage when I saw a thin wisp of smoke rising from the lamp. Gazing at it in horror, I realised the tassels at the bottom of the shade had caught fire.

What should I do?

For a long second, I froze, then, sensing the audience's eyes burning into my back, I bent over and pretended to tidy the items on the table. As I lowered my head, I puffed hard at the burning tassels.

One went out, but the others only blazed more brightly. Sucking in a quick breath, I puffed again. And again. And again. Thank God! Finally, they were all out.

Trying desperately to regain my composure, I stood up, flicked my feather duster and walked offstage.

Bob was standing in the wings watching me and I burst into nervous giggles as soon as I reached him.

"That was terrible!" I whispered. "I thought I was going to set the whole theatre on fire! Do you think the audience noticed?"

Bob grinned.

"To hell with the audience. What am I going to tell my wife? That's her favourite lampshade!"

The words hit me like a bucket of ice. My wife.

I felt sick. I tried to tell myself I was being ridiculous. Bob and I were just friends. We were members of the same club. What difference did it make that he was married?

I tried hard to lie to myself but, deep down, I knew the truth.

It mattered because I was in love with him.

That night, as soon as the curtain came down, I made an excuse about being tired and went home. In my bedroom, I buried my face in my pillow and sobbed myself to sleep.

I didn't want anyone to know what an idiot I had been, so I tried even harder than usual to keep my emotions hidden.

Over the following months, I kept going to the club and was involved in every production. Sometimes I managed to win a small part, but mostly I helped with the lighting or the sound or worked backstage.

At home, the circus was finally coming together. David invited many of the club members to see what we were making, and news of our strange obsession began to spread. Most of the model was built from recycled materials, and over the years, our neighbours had helped us by passing on old clocks or mechanical toys that Dad could strip down for cogwheels.

Now, we began to find bags of broken toys, copper tubing and even a huge jar of decorative buttons left on our doorstep by well-wishers.

David invited Bob to visit one evening and he was captivated by the circus. I listened as he asked Dad what he planned to do with the model.

"When it's finished, we're going to put it on exhibition," Dad explained.

"When will that be?"

"I'm not sure," Dad replied. "There's still a lot to do."

"I wouldn't wait, if I were you. I think it's incredible as it is. People will love it."

His eyes were sparkling as he admired the tiny horses Dad was making and I struggled to hide a rush of emotion.

Since we had finished the play together, I had avoided being alone with Bob and I sensed that he, in turn, had been keeping his distance from me. I was afraid he must have thought me very rude.

Whenever I had the chance, I watched him from a distance, and I listened out for any conversations or snippets of gossip about him.

I was surprised to find that he was twenty-two years older than me. He felt more "my age" than anyone I knew. It also came as a shock when I realised that his eldest daughter was only a year younger than me.

There was something about Bob that made him the life and soul of the group. He was good-looking and had an easy charm that made him universally liked. I also realised I wasn't the only one who found him attractive. Most of the female club members had a crush on him and there was a lot of speculation about his home life.

It hadn't struck me as odd before, but I began to see that

between his job, which involved long hours travelling, and his time spent at the club, he could hardly ever be at home.

Just before Christmas, another local drama club invited our members to join them for a disco. It was a great night, and I was spinning around on the dance floor when I turned and found myself face to face with Bob.

Our eyes met and, in that instant, I saw that his feelings for me were as strong as mine were for him. At once, my whole world changed. I knew, without a doubt, that Bob and I would spend the rest of our lives together, but I dreaded the thought of what that would involve.

The next three years were the unhappiest of my life.

Bob separated from his wife and moved into a flat. He was well known around Exeter, and rumours and gossip spread like wildfire.

Once the divorce process started, Bob worried about the effect the changes would have on his daughters and every stage dragged on for months. Life became a series of hurdles to be overcome.

As time passed, it dawned on me that my hopes and dreams for the future had changed.

I still wanted to act and create things, and I desperately wanted to finish the circus, but the most important thing in my life was to be with Bob. I couldn't imagine life without him. One day, it dawned on me that, even if I had been offered a place at the best drama school in the country, I wouldn't have accepted it if it meant moving away.

I couldn't make sense of my emotions. What had happened to me? I had always been so logical. If this was love, then I wasn't sure I liked it.

And yet, at the same time, I was happier than I had ever been. Despite all the difficulties we faced, I had a simple conviction that somehow, one day, everything would work out for the best.

Linda, Bob's eldest daughter, had left home before I met him, but as soon as he was settled into his new flat, she moved in with him.

Linda was blonde, bubbly, and vivacious. She had clear opinions on every subject and had no hesitation in sharing them. Much to my relief, she was not upset by my relationship with her dad and told me she was glad to see him happy.

Penny, his youngest, was still in school, and I had met her several times at the club. She was a quiet, pretty girl with a wide smile like her father, and I knew it meant a lot to Bob that we should get on. I liked Penny, but because she was also quiet by nature, we had never had a proper conversation.

Once the divorce was finalised, Bob suggested he take Penny and me out for Sunday lunch in a pub so that we could get to know each other.

I was afraid the meeting would be painfully awkward, but I knew it was important. I made a great effort to dress properly for the occasion. Instead of my usual jeans, I wore an itchy wool skirt, roll-neck jumper and leather boots. I had a vague idea that it might make me look grown-up.

Penny smiled at me as we sat at a table waiting for our meal. Neither of us knew what to say. Bob returned from the bar with drinks and three bags of crisps.

As I pulled my bag of crisps open, I must have been a little heavy-handed because the packet tore from top to bottom and the entire contents flew into the air and cascaded down across the table.

Penny looked at me in amazement.

Mortified, I tried to scrape the crisps together and shove them back into the remnants of the bag.

"Don't worry," Bob grinned. "I'll get you some more."

I had just finished picking the crumbs from my skirt when Bob returned.

"Here you are," he said and handed me another packet.

"Thanks," I said gratefully.

I took the packet, tore open the top and, once more, showered crisps everywhere.

Penny giggled and my cheeks burned with embarrassment.

"I'm so sorry," I said to Bob.

"Don't worry. Here, you'd better have mine. They're already open."

The pub was particularly busy that day and we had to wait a long time to be served. I soon finished my cider and Bob asked if I would like another.

"Yes, please."

Penny told me a little about her school while Bob was at the bar ordering a round of drink,s and when he returned, he handed me a new bottle of cider.

The top had already been removed, so I took the bottle in my right hand, intending to pour it into the glass I was holding in my left hand.

Unfortunately, my nerves got the better of me and, instead of pouring the cider into my glass, I poured the entire half pint straight into my lap.

This time, Penny couldn't control herself and burst into peals of laughter.

~

"That was a disaster," I said to Bob when we had dropped Penny back to her mother's house.

"Not really," he assured me. "She likes you. She said you're totally nuts, but she likes you."

I was relieved that Linda and Penny accepted me, but I was concerned that I had not yet met Julia, Bob's middle daughter. I knew he had invited her on several occasions and I was worried she had not agreed to come.

My biggest concern, however, was how my parents were going to react to our relationship.

Against all the odds, I had managed to keep everything a secret from them. Bob had wanted to tell them about us as soon as his divorce went through, but I had begged him to wait.

I knew Mum would never consider Bob to be a suitable partner for me. We couldn't keep our secret forever, but I was dreading what would happen when we finally broke the news.

One evening, as Mum was sewing and Dad and I were busy with various pieces of circus modelling, David arrived home with a huge grin on his face.

"You're looking pleased with yourself," Mum said.

"I've got some news," David beamed. "I've just asked Philippa to marry me. And she said yes!"

"That's wonderful! Have you set a date?" Mum asked eagerly.

"Don't worry, it won't be for ages yet. We'll have to save up first."

Impulsively, while everyone was in a happy mood, and Mum and I were in the kitchen preparing a celebratory pot of tea, I blurted out that I, too, had some news.

"What's that, dear?" she asked as she arranged chocolate fingers on a plate.

"I'm going to get married as well."

Mum froze.

"What do you mean? Who to?"

"Bob Townsend," I said in a rush.

As soon as the words were out, I regretted them. Mum's face blanched.

"You can't," she said. "He's so.... old."

"No, he's not!" I protested. "I love him, Mum. Can't you just be happy for me?"

I could see from her expression that she was anything but happy.

"We're not going to talk about this now," she said as she turned away. "It's not fair to spoil this moment for your brother."

~

I had known Mum and Dad would be upset, but I was shocked by how badly they reacted to my news. Mum cried for days and Dad retreated to his workshop at the bottom of the garden.

I had never felt so miserable.

I tried to persuade my parents that I was not about to ruin my life, but they would not listen.

Mum begged me to change my mind. She cried and pleaded, telling me stories of girls she had known who had married older men with disastrous results.

"It will end in tears," she warned me. "It's not too late. Just tell him you've changed your mind."

~

Over the next year, there were lots of heated arguments and tearful exchanges. Dad gradually accepted that I was not going to change my mind, but Mum was stubbornly determined to make me see sense. It would have been easy to walk out and move in with Bob, but I knew I would never be happy unless I found a way to make things right with her.

"You've got your whole life ahead of you," Mum said yet again.

"I know," I replied patiently, "and I'm going to spend it with Bob."

"But why? I can't understand what you see in him."

"He's kind and thoughtful and he makes me happy. Isn't that what you want? For me to be happy?"

"You know it is, darling, but I wish you weren't so obstinate. You should be planning your life with someone your own age."

I wanted to tell her it was not Bob's age that mattered, but I didn't know how to explain. The truth was that it was her age that was worrying me.

I loved my mother very much and she was a remarkable woman. She had travelled twice around the world and had supported her family from the money she earned from her writing long before she met Dad. She was strong and brave and resilient. I didn't just love her, I admired her, but she and Dad were already well into their sixties.

I wanted to be with Bob, but I also wanted much more. I dreamed of having a family of our own and I wanted our kids to be born soon so that they would have a chance to grow up knowing their grandparents.

I wish now that I had tried to explain my thinking to Mum, but at the time, I was afraid I wouldn't be able to find the right words.

Mum sniffed again, and I sensed that more tears were on their way.

Turning away from her, I headed into the kitchen, filled the kettle yet again, and wondered if it was possible to overdose on tea.

Dad was by the sink.

"You have to be patient with her," he said quietly. "If she didn't love you, she wouldn't be so be worried about you."

"I know she loves me, but I'm not a kid anymore. I'm twenty-two."

"It doesn't make any difference." Dad sighed. "You'll understand one day. Being a parent is forever. To her, you will always be her baby daughter and she will always know what's best for you. Come here."

I leaned against him, and he gave me a great big bearhug.

Like most girls, I had always dreamed of falling in love and having a wonderful fairytale wedding, but now, I realised that would not be possible.

While David and Philippa spent their evenings planning guest lists and choosing bridesmaid's dresses, I searched for a way that Bob and I could get married with the least possible fuss.

David's birthday is in early March and I persuaded Bob that if we arranged a huge birthday party for him and invited everyone we knew, then, once everyone was assembled, we could simply announce that we had got married that afternoon.

We kept the service itself as simple as possible. A quick trip to the registry office with only my parents, David, Philippa, and Bob's three daughters, as guests.

It was not the way I had wanted things to be, but all I cared about was being able to marry Bob without causing any more grief.

I had still not come to terms with the idea of being a stepmother. Since she had moved in with her father, Linda and I saw a lot of each other and she found the idea of me being her step-mother hysterically funny.

Penny didn't seem bothered by the idea, but I still had no idea how Julia felt. Bob had invited her over for a meal on many occasions, but she always made an excuse, and I was convinced she must hate me.

When I heard she had accepted her invitation to the wedding, I began to panic. What if she was only coming to object? One night I woke up in a sweat, dreaming I was being chased around the registry office by a strange woman with a knife. I knew I was being ridiculous, so I pushed my fears to the back of my mind.

Finally, the day of the wedding arrived, and I dressed in a simple white skirt and blouse topped by a blue velvet coat I had borrowed from my mother. I felt extremely nervous, but I was also excited that I was finally going to build a life with the man I loved.

For the first time ever, I was ready on time.

As I walked into the registry office, Bob and his daughters were waiting for me. They were all smiling, and Julia was friendly and welcoming. Not a knife in sight.

The rest of the day was perfect. Mum and Dad managed to keep smiling, and every time I caught Bob's eye, I knew we were doing the right thing.

In the evening, when Bob stood up and made our surprise announcement, there was a stunned silence followed by a wave of congratulations and applause. The relief was huge. I felt as though a great weight had been lifted from me and, finally, I could be happy.

The first day of a long and happy marriage.

CHAPTER 6

A few weeks later, David and Phil tied the knot in a beautiful church ceremony, and when they returned from their honeymoon, we settled down for yet another pot of tea.

The circus was nearing completion. We could have gone on adding to it forever, but we all agreed it had reached a stage where it was ready to be put on exhibition to the public.

David and I were still working full time in the family printing business, and we both hated it. Dad was nearly sixty-eight and his headaches were not improving. Mum was worried the fumes from the inks we used might be triggering some of them, and we all felt we needed to find a new way to earn a living. But were we chasing an impossible dream? Could anyone really support themselves by exhibiting a model circus?

There was only one way to find out. After an emotional family meeting, we decided to take the plunge. We closed the printing business and looked for a suitable place to show the circus.

After much searching, we hired part of an ancient

building known as the Spanish Barn on Torquay seafront. We designed posters, handed them out around the town, and opened our model to the public.

On the first morning, we opened the doors and held our breath. Would anyone come? Would they think our circus was worth the entrance money? We could hardly look at each other as we waited.

Shortly after ten, the first family arrived, paid their money and disappeared behind the screen to view the circus. Others soon followed them. Eventually, the first family emerged and came back to the ticket box. I could feel Mum tense as we watched them approach. Were they going to demand their money back?

"I wanted to ask about the circus," the woman began. "It's wonderful, absolutely beautiful. Can you tell us who made it?"

Mum and I breathed a sigh of relief. We were on our way.

~

Within a few weeks, it was clear we had made the right decision. We were not making a fortune, but we quickly made enough to cover our expenses, and during the peak of the summer, we took enough money to see us through the winter to the next spring.

For our second season, we hired the whole of the Spanish Barn and filled the additional space with a collection of miniature scenes and displays. Silvers Model Circus became Silvers Model World.

Unfortunately, there was a limit to how much we could build during the winter and, as we assembled the new displays in the spring, there was still a huge empty space in the middle of the barn.

At that point, Bob was running his own video business, but in the past, he had spent years in retail management.

"What you need is a gift shop," he said as he looked around the old building.

"That would be great," I agreed, "but we don't have any stock."

Bob smiled.

"No problem. I know lots of wholesalers. I could arrange it for you if you like."

"Really? That sounds awesome, but I'll have to talk to the others."

"Brilliant!" David gasped, and Dad nodded happily.

Mum was less enthusiastic. She had still not reconciled herself to having Bob as a son-in-law.

"It sounds like a big risk to me. We'd have to pay a fortune for all the stock. And what would happen if it didn't sell?"

"Don't worry," I reassured her. "Bob says he can get a whole range of stuff on sale or return so there won't be any risk and he can even arrange about all the display stands."

"It has to be worth a try," Dad agreed.

"And it would look great when people first come in," Philippa added.

"I see. Well, it looks as if I'm outvoted then." Mum sniffed.

"I'm afraid it does." I grinned. "I'll tell Bob to get everything sorted."

The whole family outside the Spanish Barn

The gift shop was a huge success and nearly doubled our takings for the year.

Bob popped in once a week with new stock to keep everything topped up and sometimes took my place at the till to give me a break.

I still didn't enjoy dealing with the public, but Bob was a natural. He had an easy way of chatting with people and I noticed the takings were always higher when he was behind the counter.

Our second year filled us with confidence. It was wonderful to see visitors enjoying our displays, and we found the circus was developing a reputation of its own. It was featured on both local and national television, and as its fame spread, our visitor numbers steadily increased and we extended our opening hours into the evening.

Bob's business, making corporate videos, involved a lot of travel, so, during the summer, we hardly ever saw each other.

One evening, after I returned from Torquay, I sat on the sofa and waited for Bob to get home.

"Why, it's my wife!" he grinned as he bustled through the door with a camera case slung over his shoulder and a tripod tucked under his arm. "I'd nearly forgotten what she looks like!"

"Sit down," I said as he bent down to kiss me. "We need to talk."

"That sounds serious."

"It is. I have some news."

"Oh?"

He eyed me apprehensively as he sat down.

"You're going to be a daddy again."

"Really?" His eyes opened wide and a huge smile lit his face. "That's fantastic!"

"You are pleased, aren't you?"

"Of course I am! It's wonderful."

He wrapped his arms around me, but as we kissed, he sensed my apprehension and pulled back.

"But what about you? I thought this was what you wanted?"

"Of course it is," I agreed. "It's exactly what I want, but now that it's actually happening, I'm not sure how it's going to work."

"What do you mean?"

"Well, we hardly see each other as it is."

"That's true, but you'll have more time now, won't you?"

"More time?"

"I'm sure your family won't expect you to keep going down to Torquay every day..."

"What do you mean?" I cut across him.

"If you're pregnant. You won't want to work full time, will you?"

I was shocked.

"Why not? I've spent years building the circus, more than half my life, and it's just starting to be a success. I'm not stepping back now."

"OK, don't jump on me. If that's what you want, we'll find a way to make it work."

He brushed a strand of hair away from my face and kissed me again. "Don't worry, darling, everything's going to be perfect."

~

"How did your parents take the news?" Bob asked when I got home the following night.

"Dad was pleased. He's going to be a wonderful granddad."

"And you're Mum?"

"You know what she's like." I sighed. "She made the right noises, but she couldn't quite make them convincing."

"What do you mean?"

"She would never admit it, but I think, deep down, she was still hoping that I would see sense and get a divorce."

"Charming!"

"Don't take it personally. It's really not about you. She always liked you before we got together."

Bob's face betrayed his hurt.

"It's hard not to take it personally."

"I know, but she will come around eventually. I'm sure she will."

By the beginning of December 1984, Mum had accepted her new role as a grandmother and was delighted to meet baby Claire when she was born.

Claire was very cute and I think she must have inspired David and Phil because it was exactly nine months after her arrival that Phil gave birth to Michael.

Our little family had expanded to eight.

The following winter, we built yet more models, bought new lines for the gift shop, and even considered selling cream teas, but, as the Spanish Barn had no running water or toilets, we soon realised that was a non-starter.

In fact, the lack of facilities in the barn was becoming a real problem. The nearest toilets were at Torre Abbey, which was a considerable distance away and something of an inconvenience.

The summer seasons were working well for us, but they seemed to grow shorter each year as visitors flew abroad for their holidays in the spring and autumn. We discussed the possibility of keeping the Spanish Barn open in the winter, but we knew there would not be enough trade to justify the expense.

"Well, if the mountain won't go to Mohammad…" Bob said mysteriously.

"What do you mean?" I asked him.

"It's simple," Bob replied. "If there's no winter trade in Torquay, you need to move the exhibition somewhere else."

"How on earth could we do that?" I asked.

"I'm not talking about moving the whole exhibition, just the circus and the gift shop. You could hire a unit in a shopping centre and maybe add a Santa's Grotto for the run up to Christmas."

I grinned.

"That sounds awesome! I can't wait to tell the others."

"Out of the question!" Mum's voice was shrill with indignation. "He has no idea what he's talking about. We can't just pick everything up and move it!"

"Why not?" Dad was as calm as ever. "The circus was made to travel, and everything from the shop could be packed into boxes."

"And it could be a great money earner," David said excitedly. "Christmas is the biggest time of the year for gifts and having a Santa's Grotto would bring loads of families in."

"But how much would it cost?" Mum wailed. "It would be a huge risk."

"We'll need to cost it all out," Dad agreed, "but it could be just what we need."

"You really have stirred things up this time," I told Bob when I got home. "Everyone thinks the Christmas season is a great idea. Everyone except Mum. I think she wants to kill you."

"Really?" Bob grinned mischievously. "In that case, maybe I'll come with you. It's only going to be for six weeks, after all."

Bob was as good as his word and arranged for us to hire a disused unit in a shopping centre in Basingstoke. It was enormous. I had anticipated a space similar to the Spanish Barn, but this was at least ten times bigger.

"You're mad!" I said when Bob showed me a ground plan of the unit. "We'll never fill all that!"

"Don't panic," Bob grinned. "We can put up some partitions and only use the space we need."

"But what's the point in paying for all that and then not using it?"

Bob looked pleased with himself.

"That's the beauty of it. We don't have to pay a penny."

"What do you mean?"

"The council in Basingstoke usually pays to have a Christmas display in the town centre, but this year they're a bit short of cash. When I approached them and offered to take the circus there and build a lovely grotto, they were so keen to have it as a Christmas attraction they agreed not to charge us any rent. Everyone's happy. They get a free attraction and we get a free unit. Win, win."

"I don't believe it! That's amazing!"

"Happy now?" he grinned.

The exhibition was a huge success. Each day, queues of families waited to see the circus and Santa's Grotto, and the gift shop was packed.

One Saturday, as I sat behind a till, Bob appeared beside me. He held a phone in his hand and I could tell by his expression that something was wrong.

"You'd better take this," he said.

It was the manageress of Granny's nursing home.

"I'm afraid your grandmother has been taken ill. The doctor is with her at the moment, but we think she's had a stroke."

"Is she going to be okay?" I asked.

"I'm afraid we don't know yet. I thought you might want to pop over."

"Oh," I hesitated. "I'm afraid that's a bit difficult..."

"She really is quite ill."

"I'm sorry, I would come if I could, but it's not that easy..."

The manageress's voice grew cold.

"Well, it's entirely up to you, of course, but if you want to see her, I suggest you don't leave it too long."

"I understand," I said. "I'll be there as soon as I can."

Bob offered to go back with me, but I shook my head.

"The others won't be able to cope without both of us. I feel badly enough about leaving as it is. Are you sure you're going to be all right with Claire?"

"It's not Claire that I'm worried about," Bob said plaintively. "You're leaving me here with your mother."

His brown eyes were mournful, and I couldn't help but smile.

"Maybe this is a good time to make friends," I suggested.

It took over three hours to drive to Exeter, and by the time I reached the nursing home, it was pitch black and raining.

I rang the doorbell and listened to the heavy clink of locks being turned.

"I'm afraid you're too late," the matron said bluntly as she opened the door. "Your grandmother has passed away."

"Oh..."

The matron glared at me as I stood on the step.

"I'm sorry," I said at last and turned and walked back to the car.

I spent the night at home and drove back to Basingstoke the next morning. I was worried how Mum would react to the news, but she merely hugged me.

"I'm sorry," she said, "I shouldn't have left you to deal with Granny, but I just couldn't take any more. I don't think I would still be here if you hadn't stepped in when you did."

"It's okay."

I held her tight.

"At least it's over," Mum said quietly. "I don't think she was ever really happy in life, but maybe now she will be at peace."

"Let's hope so," I agreed.

We discussed closing for a couple of days so everyone could return home for the funeral, but we had signed an agreement with the council to open the exhibition every day until Christmas Eve and we couldn't see how we could get out of it.

"In any case," David said, "I don't want to sound callous, but it's not going to make any difference to Granny if we're there or not, is it?"

"I know," I agreed, "but it feels disrespectful."

"To be honest, I'm more concerned about Mum than about being respectful," David replied. "She's shattered already. The last thing she needs is to rush back to Exeter, have all the stress of Granny's funeral, then rush back here again."

He was right. Mum looked tired and strained. I guessed she was feeling guilty that she hadn't visited Granny since she had moved into the home.

"Maybe we should suggest she leaves everything to us."

To my surprise, Mum didn't object to letting David and me make all the arrangements for the funeral.

"I'm sorry," she said, "I know it's wrong, but I just don't have any emotion left for her. There's nothing in my heart except a big hole. If you can cope with handling things, I would be very grateful."

David gave her a huge hug.

"Of course we can. Don't upset yourself, it's not a problem."

I had never organised a funeral before, and neither had David. It was difficult being so far from home, and we were not sure where to start.

After making some phone calls, I managed to find a funeral director who explained everything we would need.

He told me he was sorry for my devastating loss and kept referring to "your dearest grandmother."

To my surprise, he asked me a barrage of questions about Granny. What was her favourite hymn? What sort of music did she like? What were her favourite flowers? Her favourite colours? Her favourite poems? I wanted to be helpful, but I had no idea about any of it.

~

David and I drew lots for who would go to the funeral. I won, or did I lose? I only remember that neither of us wanted to go.

The service was at two o'clock and I left Basingstoke early in the morning, long before the first grey streaks of dawn lightened the sky. I found myself hoping the car would break down. I imagined the relief of being towed back to Basingstoke, but the engine ran smoothly all the way to Exeter.

A crowd of tearful mourners from an earlier funeral were filing out of the chapel as I arrived.

When they had gone, I went and stood in the chapel doorway. It was a plain, angular room with magnolia walls and a brown-tiled floor covered by rows of identical wooden chairs.

To my surprise, I felt an urge to pray. When I was small, Mum had taught me to say a prayer every night before I went to sleep, but I had stopped believing in an all-seeing deity long ago. Now, as I waited for the minister to arrive, I recalled how safe I had felt kneeling beside my bed, asking God to bless my family.

The certainties of childhood felt a distant memory and tears welled up inside me that had nothing to do with my grandmother's death.

"You must be Diana." The minister's voice interrupted my thoughts. "I'm sorry I wasn't here to greet you."

"That's okay. I'm early."

"Good, good. It's always best to have time to prepare."

He was a portly man, with blue eyes, ginger hair and a pale, flabby face that balanced on his dog collar like a boiled egg on a cup.

He smiled hopefully.

"Are we expecting a big turnout?"

"No, I'm afraid not."

His smile faded.

"Never mind. I have everything prepared. Would you like to greet the mourners as they arrive, or would you rather take your place?"

"I think I'll sit down, if that's okay."

"Yes, of course it is. Whatever feels most comfortable for you."

My heels tapped as I walked to the front of the room. Respectful music floated from speakers high on the walls, and I stared into space as the minutes ticked away.

No one came.

At two o'clock, I heard the minister's footsteps behind me.

"Do you think we should give it a few more moments?" he asked, looking around at the empty seats.

"No, I don't think so," I said. I wanted to add, "We might as well get it over with," but I didn't.

The minster crossed to the lectern and was busy shuffling his papers, when the scrape of a door being opened came from the back of the room. I looked around and saw the Matron and her deputy from the nursing home.

The minister beamed at them.

"Welcome, do come down here and join us."

Ignoring him, the women sat in the back row.

There was an awkward silence and the minister's eyes flicked in my direction, but I stared straight ahead and he turned quickly back to his papers.

"Shall we sing the first hymn?" he suggested.

An electric organ played, and the minister raised his voice in a valiant attempt to fill the echoing room. A prayer was followed by a poem and a tribute to the deceased.

It was strange, sitting alone, listening to a man I did not know, telling me what a wonderful woman my grandmother had been. I had sent him an outline of her life and he had filled in the gaps with love and affection. I doubted whether Granny would have recognised herself from his words, but they stirred in me a realisation of what might have been.

In a different life, I would have been grieving for a beloved grandmother. The room would have been filled with family, friends and acquaintances who had known her and wanted to mark her passing.

Surrounded by others, I would have been wracked by sadness and loss but buoyed up by a lifetime of happy memories.

Instead, I felt hollow, devoid of any emotion except a nagging guilt. I couldn't help wondering if, in some way, it was my fault Granny had been the way she was. If I had loved her more, would she have been different?

I pushed the thought away. I was being ridiculous. No sensible person would have held me responsible and yet, deep down, I knew I was right to feel guilty. I felt guilty because I was glad she was dead.

I repeated the words of the Lord's Prayer after the minister, and when he finished, I wiped my eyes and turned around.

The Matron and her deputy had gone.

CHAPTER 7

Once Christmas was over, we brought the circus and the remains of the gift shop stock back home and started preparing for the new season.

Bob had enjoyed his time in Basingstoke, and for me, it had been a dream come true, being able to work with him every day. I didn't want to go back to being separated from him for long periods while he was away making videos.

Hesitantly, I asked if he would be able to help out sometimes in the Barn during the summer, and to my surprise, he agreed.

"But what about your parents? I'm not sure your mother will like the idea."

"She didn't mind you being in Basingstoke, did she? Maybe she's getting used to having you around?"

"Only because we were so busy, she never had to talk to me. Mostly, she just ignored me."

The next time I had a few moments alone with Mum and Dad, I mentioned that Bob had offered to help out during the summer when we were busy. They exchanged glances.

"What is it?" I asked. "What's the matter?"

For once, Dad looked serious.

"As it happens, we were talking about Bob just now."

"Why? What were you saying?"

"Nothing bad," he said quickly, "but as you and Phil both have babies to look after now, it will be more difficult to manage this summer. We were thinking we would need some extra help."

"Exactly, so that's okay then...."

Mum held up a hand.

"It's not as simple as that. We were talking about how exactly we should handle it."

"Handle what?"

"This has always been a family business, you know that," Dad said. "When David turned eighteen and started working with us, we made him a partner and we did the same for you and then for Phil when she married David. Well, if Bob wants to join us and work as part of the team, we would like to make the same offer to him."

"You mean you want him to join the business?"

"Yes," Dad said simply. "He's one of the family now, so if he wants to join, he should be a partner like the rest of us."

I was speechless. I stared from one to the other of them, uncertain how to react.

"Are you sure?" I asked at last.

Mum looked straight into my eyes.

"Of course we are. We wouldn't suggest it if we weren't sure, would we?"

"But... I mean, well, you don't exactly… like him, do you?"

"I never said that I don't like him." Mum managed to sound offended. "I've always liked him. That doesn't change the fact that he is completely unsuited to be your husband."

"Oh, my God, Mum," I gasped. "You are impossible!"

Bob was as taken aback by my parents' offer as I had been.

"But I already have a business," he protested. "I thought you were talking about helping out now and again, not making a full-time commitment."

"I know. It came as a surprise to me, too. You don't have to make a decision straight away. Why don't you just think about it?"

~

After the relative freedom of running the exhibition in Basingstoke, the restrictions of working in a listed building were becoming increasingly frustrating.

After three years in The Spanish Barn, we had filled all the available space with models and there was no room to expand.

As well as the lack of facilities, we were not allowed to attach signs to the outside of the Barn or have any exterior lighting, which meant we couldn't open in the evenings. The nearest car park was a long walk away and there was no dropping-off point for coaches.

We had grown to love the old barn, but now we agreed that, if we were to continue developing our attraction, we were going to have to find a new site.

At first, it seemed easy. We contacted estate agents and explained we were looking for a large property that could be developed as a tourist attraction. We were not particularly fussy. We would consider anything as long as it had plenty of space. We would even consider buying a property if there was nothing available to rent. Surely there must be lots of places that would suit us?

After months of searching, our optimism faded. We looked at all sorts of properties, old churches, hotels, farm buildings, even a former ice-cream factory, but nothing was suitable.

I was beginning to feel distinctly depressed when a phone

call came through from an estate agent. He had heard of a property that was about to come onto the market and wondered if we might be interested. It was at Chudleigh, just outside Exeter, but he had no details. He only knew that it had last been used as a school and would be within our price range.

There was nothing in his description that made the property sound any better or worse than those we had already visited, but for some inexplicable reason, I felt a tingle of anticipation. I was convinced this place was going to be special.

The others agreed the property sounded interesting, so I phoned back and arranged for us to go and see it that evening.

All day long, I was filled with a bubbling excitement. It was a lovely sunny day in late May and the Barn was not due to close until six o'clock. Usually, I would be happy to stay open for a few extra minutes while the last customers browsed in the gift shop, but tonight, I made up the till and waited impatiently for them to go.

We had recently bought a minibus to cope with our expanding family and, as soon as the Barn doors were locked, we strapped the babies into their seats and headed off towards Chudleigh.

The early evening light was warm and golden as we followed the agent's directions along the Teign Valley. Bob was driving the minibus and beside him I peered through the windscreen, anxious to catch the first glimpse of the old school.

As instructed, we left the A38, followed a smaller road, and turned into a private drive. After a few moments, we pulled up at a gate barring our way and stared ahead.

The scene before us was beyond anything we had been expecting, and we looked at each other uncertainly.

"Are you sure this is the right place?" Dad asked at last.

"Well..." Bob hesitated. "The directions seem clear enough..."

"But there must be some mistake," Mum cut in. "This place is enormous."

Beyond the gate, the drive continued towards a distant building. It looked like a stately home, with Georgian bow windows, elegant carved verandas and an impressive bell tower topping the ornate roof. Behind it, chimneys and gables suggested other buildings set farther up the hill.

"Should we go in?" I asked doubtfully, but at that moment, a Range Rover pulled up behind us.

An energetic young man in a flashy suit climbed out and hurried to open the gate.

"Glad you found the place all right. I'm Nick Stevens, by the way. Park up by the house somewhere and I'll show you round."

Without a word, Bob guided the minibus through the gate and followed the drive to the house. As we got closer, it became obvious the old building had been neglected for many years. Lengths of guttering hung at crazy angles. Sections of render had fallen from the walls and lay in crumbling piles on the ground, revealing gaping patches of stonework like open wounds. Here and there, windows were broken and slipping tiles spoiled the symmetry of the roof.

Stokelake House

We climbed out of the minibus and stared around us. No

one seemed to know what to say. We strapped the babies into their buggies as the Range Rover roared up and Nick Stevens got out.

"I'm afraid I don't have any details for you right now," he apologised. "I think my secretary explained that Stokelake House isn't officially on the market yet, but we should have everything sorted in a couple of days and if you're interested, I can post the paperwork on to you then."

He paused, obviously expecting a reaction, but when no one spoke, he ploughed on regardless.

"Normally, of course, I would let you in by the front door, but I'm afraid we haven't received the keys yet. I only have the set the security firm has been using, so I'm afraid I'll have to let you in by a side door. Follow me, please."

He set off at a brisk pace and we followed him, gazing at the wild expanse of meadow which must once have been a lawn, or trying to catch glimpses of the rooms that lay behind the dirty windows. We came to a large clump of laurel bushes and I was astounded to see that another section of building stretched ahead of us.

Dad shook his head in disbelief.

"This is crazy," he muttered.

Nick pulled open a gate that was obscured by the laurels and ushered us into a small yard.

"How long is it since the school closed?" David asked as Nick struggled to unlock an ancient door.

"Oh, about seven or eight years, I think. The history of the building is a bit complicated, I'm afraid."

"And it's been left empty all that time?" Dad frowned.

"As far as I know," Nick managed to force the door open. "There. You can have a look round if you like, but be a bit careful, I'm not sure what state the place might be in."

He held the door wide for us but made no move to go in himself.

"You mean you haven't been over the property yourself?" Bob asked.

"Not yet," Nick replied breezily.

"I think I'd better stay here with the children," Mum said. "The rest of you can take a look if you want."

I hesitated. It was clear everyone was overawed by the sheer size and condition of the old school, but the tingle of anticipation I had felt earlier had only grown stronger. Even in its present state, there was something undeniably beautiful about Stokelake House. There was a gentle elegance about its architecture that shone through the dirt and neglect. It was like a magnificent painting that needed only to be stripped of dirt and varnish to be able to dazzle once again.

"Well, we might as well look now we're here," I said and stepped through the doorway into the dark corridor beyond. The others followed me.

The corridor turned to the right and I gasped. Ahead of me was an enormous kitchen. Along one wall stretched a row of gas ovens and along another was a series of steel sinks the size of baths. I wondered how many children the school had catered for.

Beyond the kitchen, another corridor led back towards the front of the house. Doors led off into empty rooms with bare floorboards and peeling walls. It was already beginning to get dark, so I flicked a light switch. Nothing happened.

Bob caught up with me as I turned a corner and stepped into the main entrance hall.

"Wow! Look at this," I gasped.

It was magnificent. Or at least it had been. A sweeping staircase led up to a galleried landing and the ceiling was rich with ornate plaster mouldings.

Only the walls betrayed the damage of its recent use. Broken laths jutted from holes kicked in the plaster and older wounds had been roughly patched with pieces of board or plywood.

"It's incredible."

Bob pushed open a door and stepped into a large, well-proportioned room that was dominated by a huge bay window looking out across the grounds. It was completely empty except for a broken chair and a cardboard box of old newspapers that spilled out across the floor.

"Let's have a look upstairs," I urged, "before it gets too dark to see."

We tiptoed up the staircase, testing the steps carefully as we went, but everything seemed sound. Then we explored, hurrying from room to room. The ceilings here were lower than downstairs, but the rooms were still light and well proportioned. I guessed they had originally been bedrooms, but there was no sign of furniture, only dusty floorboards and a scattering of dead flies. Here and there, dark patches on the ceilings showed where rainwater had seeped through.

"Perhaps we'd better go and find the others," Bob suggested.

"What?" I turned abruptly and was surprised to find we were alone. I had been sure David, Phil, and Dad were right behind us, and for a moment, the feeling lingered.

I turned around, checking the corners of the room. We were definitely alone, but I couldn't shake the feeling that the somebody was close by.

"Hello!" I called. "We're in here."

"Who are you talking to?" Bob was grinning at me. "Didn't you notice? The others found another door out of the kitchen."

"No, I missed that." I was clearly making a fool of myself. I made a mental note not to let my imagination run away with me.

"Let's go a bit farther. We must be nearly at the end of this part of the house."

I stepped back into the corridor and followed it as it turned again to the left.

"Oh, my God!"

Ahead of me, a staircase led upwards, another led down to the ground floor, and a dim corridor stretched into the distance.

Bob stared over my shoulder. "There's another whole wing. Good grief, how big is this place?"

I didn't answer. Outside, the sun was setting, and the shadows were growing deeper. Inside, patches of gloomy darkness gathered in corners and I found myself staring into them.

"I think we'd better go and find the others," Bob repeated, and this time I agreed.

We felt our way back down the staircase and paused at the bottom. Ahead of us we could hear voices.

"Is that you?" I shouted.

"Come and see what we've found!" Phil called back excitedly.

We followed the sound of her voice and found ourselves back outside the kitchen. David was holding open a huge door that looked a little like the entrance to a bank vault.

"What is it?" I asked.

"Guess."

I stared. The heavy door opened into a windowless room about the size of my bathroom at home. A single light bulb hung from the ceiling.

"Some kind of safe?" I ventured.

"Wrong." David pushed past me, grinning. He picked up a pile of wooden slats lying on the floor and held one out to me. "I'll give you a clue. These should be shelves."

I shook my head, none the wiser.

"And look at these." He pointed up to a row of meat hooks hanging from the ceiling.

"Oh, my God! It's a freezer!"

"Yes. And look at this." Phil pulled open another door to reveal an even bigger room. "This one's a fridge. Aren't they amazing? You could store enough food for an army in here."

"And there are classrooms." David added. "If you go along that way, there are four great big classrooms and a staircase that takes you up to four more."

"Another staircase?" I turned to Bob. "That makes three, doesn't it?"

"Four if you include the one we haven't been up yet."

I was beginning to feel like Alice in Wonderland when she started to shrink and everything around her became bigger and bigger...

"We'd better make sure Mum's all right," Phil said, turning back towards the kitchen.

"Yes," I agreed. "And where's Dad?"

"Right here."

I jumped. Dad was on his hands and knees behind me. He had found a loose floorboard and was trying to prise it up with his fingers.

"What on earth are you doing?" I asked.

"Sniffing." He said, his nose brushing the dirty floor.

"I can see that, but why?"

"Dry rot. With a building of this age, you nearly always get dry rot."

"Can you smell anything?"

"No, but that doesn't mean it's not there."

The light had faded so much it was getting hard to make out people's expressions. Dad climbed to his feet and wiped his dirty hands on his trousers.

"I don't think we can see anything more tonight. How about some fish and chips?"

~

We found a fish and chip shop in the middle of Chudleigh and gathered six chairs around a table. Claire sat on my lap sucking at a chip while Michael slept in his buggy. I could barely contain my excitement.

"It's amazing! Just think what we could do with it. It's everything we've been dreaming about."

"But it's so big." Mum sounded worried. "It must be ten times the size of anything else we've seen. They must have made a mistake with the price."

I shook my head.

"No. I checked with that Nick bloke. He said the price he'd given us was definitely right."

"It can't be. They must have left a nought off the end or something."

"It does seem way out of line with anything else we've looked at," Bob agreed.

Dad shook a blizzard of salt across his chips. "Maybe there's a good reason for the price being so low."

"You mean dry rot?"

"Possibly. Or subsidence. Or there's a plan for a motorway to go right through the middle of it. Or it's built over old mines...."

"But that's all rubbish!" I protested. "What if there's nothing wrong with it? Just think what it could be like."

"But what would we do about the field?" David asked.

"It wouldn't be a field, would it?" I retorted. "Imagine how beautiful it would be if it was all lawns and flowerbeds instead of blackberries and nettles. And think about the house for a minute. We could have different exhibitions in every part of it. We could have a special room just for the circus and proper tearooms and everything."

"But what exhibitions are you talking about?" Mum was not going to be convinced so easily. "The models we've got at the moment would only fill a couple of rooms. What on earth would we do with the rest of it?"

"David's got loads of stuff from the First World War," Phil suggested. "Maybe he could do an exhibition about that."

It was true. David was a born collector. While other little boys had been obsessed with football or rockets, he had always been fascinated by militaria. While he was still in junior school, he had befriended all the junk shop owner in Exeter and spent every penny of his pocket money on helmets, uniforms or insignia.

I can still remember the look of horror on Mum's face the day he arrived home from school with a huge Japanese sword strapped across the handlebars of his bicycle.

"That's a brilliant idea!" David exclaimed. "We could block in the windows and make some scenes to show what life was like in the trenches and then we could..."

"I'm not being a wet blanket," Dad interrupted, "but how much do you think it's going to cost to renovate a property like that? It'll probably need a new roof to start with. There's water coming through everywhere. Have you any idea how much that would cost? And the outside would need to be re-rendered, and there's the electrics and the plumbing..."

He paused and looked around at us. "And after all that, the whole place would have to be decorated. Just imagine how much carpet it would take to start with. Acres of it. I just don't see how we could find that kind of money."

He was right. I knew he was right, but I didn't want to let go of my dream.

"But what if it doesn't need a new roof?" I pleaded. "It might not be as bad as it looks, or we could borrow the money, or find a partner or something. Surely we should at least try?"

There was a strained silence.

"Well, I guess we can't make any decisions tonight," Dad said at last. "Perhaps we should come back for another look once we've got the full details."

We all murmured our agreement.

"And next time," David added, "we'd better bring some torches."

Looking back, it's hard to believe how naive we were when we first viewed Stokelake House. We had absolutely no idea what we were taking on. We knew nothing of planning regulations, building regulations, health and hygiene certification, health and safety rulings or fire prevention officers.

We had no policies, procedures or accreditations. We had never heard of risk assessments, or even cash flow projections.

All we had was optimism, enthusiasm, and belief.

After all, this was 1986. The Age of the Entrepreneur when anything was possible. Margaret Thatcher had been in power for seven years and Britain was booming. Ordinary people were starting businesses everywhere. In the past, people had wanted the security of jobs that took them from the cradle to the grave, but the days of union control were over. Now it was possible to buy your own council house and start your own business. Thatcher's children were coming of age and if everyone else was living their dream, then why shouldn't we?

I was certain that if we just went ahead, worked hard and put everything we had into our dream, then somehow, we would find a way to overcome the obstacles. I knew it.

And also, there was something about the old building that touched me. I couldn't explain what it was. I don't think I knew myself, and I would have felt incredibly stupid if I had had to put my feelings into words, but there was definitely something that made me feel welcome.

From the first time I stepped inside, despite the damp and the dirt and the neglect, despite the holes kicked in the walls and the dead rats in the cellars, despite everything, there was a peace about the place that calmed me. I wanted to be there. I wanted to be a part of it.

It felt like home.

~

As with everything connected to Stokelake House, the estate agent's details proved surprising. They arrived in a bulky parcel. The details themselves were scant, but Nick had included a set of plans with the note, "I thought you might find these interesting."

There were fifteen plans in all. Each had been drawn by a firm of London architects and folded out like a map. They were huge and showed intricate layouts of walls and rooms with floor plans, elevations and existing and proposed utilities.

We gazed at them without understanding what we were seeing.

Dad frowned.

"These must have cost a fortune. Why would anyone go to so much expense?"

~

The next time we visited Stokelake House, we pressed Nick to explain why the old building had been left empty.

"It's all rather complicated," he began. "In fact, I'm not sure if I've got the whole story, but apparently the school here was for, how shall I put it? Difficult children. Naughty boys if you like. The ones that other institutions couldn't handle."

"You mean it was a Borstal?" Mum asked.

"Well, not exactly." Nick seemed uncomfortable. "But let's just say they had some very troubled children here. Anyway, I think the man that ran the schools — he had two others — decided he'd had enough. I'm not sure what the reasoning was behind it, but he closed all the schools at the same time.

This site was put up for sale, and of course, at that time, the estate was still intact."

"What estate?" Bob asked.

Nick turned to face him.

"The estate that went with the house. When it was first built, Stokelake House had an estate of over 300 acres. Any house of this size would have had an estate in those days."

"So, they sold the land off separately?"

"Not at first. The new owners bought the whole site and wanted to use the land for a leisure development. To be honest, I don't think they were interested in the old school at all. It just came with the package, so they left it empty and went about setting up a huge caravan site with pine lodges and a leisure centre and so on, but then, just over a year ago, they went bankrupt. Now another company has taken over and is selling everything separately. A lot of the farmland has already been sold, and the caravan park, of course, and that leaves Stokelake House itself. I think they're looking for a quick sale and that's why the property is so competitively priced."

"It's a pity they've sold off all the land," I joked. "I would have liked having a country estate!"

"Well, the house does still come with some land," Nick added quickly.

"Some?" Phil queried.

"Fifteen acres, to be precise. Didn't you notice? It's listed in the details."

We stared at each other.

"Fifteen acres?" Bob repeated blankly. "No. We hadn't noticed that."

~

Strangely, the thought of taking on fifteen acres of neglected parkland in addition to a crumbling mansion didn't worry us that much. I think by now we were all losing touch with reality. The strange old building had us under its spell.

In addition to the fifteen acres of grounds, we found the site included two large dormitory blocks, a separate building with another ten classrooms, a two-story science block, a huge indoor swimming pool with a crack from one end to the other and, right at the top of the hill, an enormous one thousand square metre sports hall.

Why we didn't come to our senses and walk away I can't imagine, but the more we saw, the more we wanted to believe in our dreams. And all this was being offered for little more than the cost of an average family home.

Even Bob, who was usually the most sceptical of us, began to see the possibilities. The classroom block was built around a small courtyard and the rooms were light and airy, with windows on both sides. Why didn't we rent them out to craftspeople as workshops, he suggested. We could have our own craft centre.

It was a brilliant idea. Visitors could watch the craftspeople at work and buy their products. It would give us another attraction and even earn a little rental income. All we had to do was repair the roofs, re-glaze the windows, and redecorate the units.

"You never did decide if you want to join the business," I said to Bob while we were getting ready for bed.

"No, I didn't," he replied. "I'm still thinking about it."

I looked at him and was relieved to see his brown eyes were wide with amusement.

"What do you think I should do?" he asked. "Should I give up my business? For a share of a derelict school? For years of hard work? For having to cope with my mother-in-law, who hates me? Do you think that's what I should do?"

"Well, only if you really want to..." I said hopefully.

I think it was David who asked whether we would need planning permission to open a craft centre. It was a simple question, but none of us knew the answer. After a short discussion, we decided the best thing was for Bob and me to visit the planning department and ask their advice. After all, they might be able to offer us some helpful suggestions.

We phoned ahead to make an appointment, and a few days later, Bob and I found ourselves sitting in the waiting area of the planning department, anticipating our meeting.

I had made out a list of questions and was feeling both excited and nervous.

A small man in a suit came towards us.

"Good afternoon," he said formally. "Your appointment is at 3 pm?"

"That's right," I began brightly. "We were hoping you could—"

"Follow me, please." He turned away abruptly and walked along a corridor, then opened the door to an office and signalled for us to enter.

We followed him obediently and sat in the chairs he indicated.

"I am Neil Turner," he said, settling himself in a chair across the desk from us, "Head of the Devon County Planning Department. Perhaps you could explain exactly what you are proposing."

I hesitated. I had a feeling I was missing something. We had come looking for help and advice. I hadn't expected to be interrogated by the head of the planning department.

Bob sensed my discomfort.

"Good to meet you, Mr Turner. I'm Robert Townsend and this is my wife, Diana. We've been looking at a property called Stokelake House. I don't know whether you've heard of it, it's near Chudleigh in the Teign Valley..."

"Yes, I know why you're here."

Mr Turner pulled open a drawer of the filing cabinet

behind him. He tugged out a thick folder bulging with papers and deposited it on the table. On the front were the words "Stokelake House" in large red letters.

"I am well acquainted with the site," he said coldly. "Now, perhaps you can tell me exactly what it is you are proposing."

I had a stupid urge to get up, walk out of the room, knock on the door, and come back in. I wanted to start again. We seemed to have got off on the wrong foot with this man, and I didn't know why.

"What we really wanted was some advice," I said and smiled at him. "We are hoping to open Stokelake House as a tourist attraction and we wanted to know where we stand from a planning point of view."

Mr Turner looked at me for a long moment as if trying to judge my sincerity, then he dropped his gaze to the file on his desk.

"You will find there is an obstacle to your plans."

"And what's that?" Bob asked.

"Stokelake House is due to be demolished. It is the intention of the planning department that the whole site be razed to the ground and returned to grassland."

~

I was still in a state of shock when we got back to the Barn. I suppose I had known our plans were incomplete and unrealistic, but I hadn't expected them to be crushed so brutally. All I wanted was to find a quiet place to cry, but instead, I had to go and break the news to the others.

As we walked into the Barn, I could see Mum had Claire with her behind the counter of the gift shop. I picked my daughter up and gave her a cuddle.

"I think you need your nappy changed, don't you?" I said before Mum could ask any questions. "I'll just take her over to the Abbey. As soon as we close, I'll tell you what happened."

~

Bob and I sat on the grass outside the Barn with Claire and waited while the others closed up.

They came across with anxious faces and sat down silently, waiting for us to explain.

"It's a long story," I began, "but I'm afraid it's bad news. We're going to have to look for somewhere else."

"But why?" David couldn't contain himself. "What's the problem? I don't see..."

"Listen," Bob said. "It's complicated. The planning man pretty much told us that we haven't got a hope. It doesn't matter what proposal we put forward, the planners will object to it. It's as simple as that."

"But why?" David demanded. "They can't just..."

"We didn't understand either," Bob continued, "so we called in at the estate agent's and had a chat with Nick's boss. He's worked around here for years and he obviously knows the whole story. To put it mildly, there are a few things Nick didn't tell us."

"Like what?"

"Well, it's a long story. It seems that while the school was open, it caused a lot of problems for the people living nearby. There was constant vandalism, petty crimes, shoplifting, even some more serious stuff like drugs and arson. Apparently, some of the locals started a campaign to have the place closed, and it got a lot of support. But it wasn't just the boys' behaviour that was the problem. During the 60s and 70s, when the school was being developed, the planning regulations weren't as strict as they are now. There were a lot of objections to the classroom block and the dormitories being built because they're so visible from the other side of the valley."

"They're not exactly beautiful," Mum agreed.

"It sounds as though some of the locals thought the guy who owned the school was a bit dodgy," Bob continued. "I don't know the background to it, but apparently he was getting a lot of government funding and it didn't matter how much people objected to his plans, the school kept on expanding. Clearly, some of the locals got really wound up about the whole thing and swore that they would find a way to get rid of the place."

"Nick's boss went a bit quiet about that," I added. "I think he knew more than he was prepared to tell us, but the next thing that happened, literally overnight, was that the school closed."

"As you can imagine, the locals were over the moon," Bob continued, "but of course, it didn't solve the problem of all the ugly buildings that had been put up."

"Anyway, it wasn't long before the school was sold and a new owner turned up. This guy wanted to develop the whole three hundred acres as a leisure resort, but when he approached the planners, they insisted there would have to be a public enquiry into any new proposals."

Bob paused for breath.

"So, to cut a long story short," I jumped in, "it was agreed that the leisure development could go ahead provided the school was demolished and the site was returned to grassland. Oh, and it all had to be completed within ten years."

"That was nine years ago," Bob continued. "The new owners went ahead with the leisure development, but they ignored the demolition part. Then they went bankrupt and everything came to a halt. The planning man was quite adamant, though. As far as the department is concerned, everything is set in stone. The whole place has to be demolished."

David tore up a handful of grass and hurled it away from him. "Well, that's it then. It's over."

A deep gloom settled over everyone. Only Michael gurgled and burped.

It was Dad who broke the silence.

"We may be giving up too soon," he said quietly. "Just think about it for a minute. What happens if we don't buy the place?"

We all waited, uncertain where he was leading.

"It's all very well the planners insisting the place has to be demolished," Dad said, "but who's going to pay for it? How much would it cost to bulldoze a place like that and return it all to pasture?"

I began to see what Dad was thinking. I had no idea what demolishing the school would cost, but it would have to be a small fortune.

"It was straightforward when the whole site belonged to one owner," Dad continued, "but we know the caravan park has already been sold. The new owners haven't bought the school, so how could the planners force them to demolish something they don't even own?"

"And if we don't buy the school because of the demolition order, then no one else will either," Phil added. "The school will probably just stand there for years, getting more and more derelict."

"Exactly," Dad agreed. "It will turn into an even worse eyesore."

"So, what are you suggesting?" I asked.

"I'm just saying that what we're proposing to do with Stokelake House might be a better option than leaving it to rot."

"Of course it is," I agreed, "but how can we convince the planners?"

CHAPTER 8

Bob and I returned to the planning department and explained that we weren't going to give up our dream without a fight.

After our initial meeting, Mr Turner seemed to have thawed a little. I got the impression Stokelake House had caused him many headaches over the years, and even the name of the place was enough to make him shudder.

He explained that after the last public enquiry, a special Stokelake House Subcommittee had been set up purely to deal with proposals for the site. Our only chance of getting the demolition order overturned was to put forward an alternative plan the subcommittee would support. It was clear he thought our chances of achieving that were something less than zero.

Our only other choice was to look for another property, but we all knew we were never going to find another opportunity like this.

"At least now we know why the price is so low," Dad said with a grin. "After all, what kind of idiot would want to buy a property with a demolition order on it?"

"A very special kind of idiot," I retorted. "One with a lot of imagination."

"Okay, then." He laughed. "You'd better put that imagination to work and come up with something stunning."

Life in the Spanish Barn continued as normal during the day, but every evening, once the children were settled, we would pool our ideas and come up with suggestions for displays and ways to utilise the old buildings.

As the summer evenings grew longer, we drove out and stood on the Chudleigh side of the valley looking across the A38 towards Stokelake. From this direction, there was no denying the school was a huge blot on the landscape. Ironically, the original mansion house was completely hidden by trees, and the only parts of the school that could be seen were flat-roofed, concrete buildings in the style that was so popular with school architects in the late 1960s. The classrooms and dormitories sprawled up the hillside in a huge expanse of jutting angles and concrete terraces.

"What can we do with that lot to make it beautiful?" Mum asked hopefully.

David snorted. "Beautiful? I think 'less offensive' is the best we can hope for."

"But that's not good enough," I protested. "We've got to convince people we can turn it into something wonderful."

"If we painted the buildings, it would make them look less scruffy," Phil said.

"Anything would be better than that sickly green," David agreed.

"I suppose they thought the colour would make it blend into the hillside," Bob said, but David snorted again.

"Well, if they did, they were wrong, weren't they?"

"We're not getting very far," I complained. "We need to come up with something creative."

"How about planting trees?" Mum suggested. "Perhaps we could hide everything behind a giant hedge."

"Maybe," I agreed doubtfully, "but it would take an awfully long time to grow enough trees to hide that lot."

"What is it that makes it so ugly?" Dad asked simply.

We stood and considered the scene.

"Personally, I think it's the flat roofs," David said at last.

"Yes." Bob nodded. "The flat roofs and the concrete terraces."

"I'm inclined to agree with you," Dad said. "So how about if we build gabled roofs on top of the flat roofs to match the main house and put flowerbeds across the terraces so we can grow plants and disguise all the concrete?"

"Wow!" I was impressed. "That really would make a difference."

"We could even include little towers to break up the line of the roofs."

"And we could still plant the trees," Mum added, "for the future."

In my mind, I saw the transformation take place. Perhaps our plans stood a chance after all.

~

The next morning, Mum and I were restocking the shelves in the gift shop when she turned to face me. "The one thing nobody's mentioned yet is how we're going to finance all this. If we're really serious, we need to get things moving."

I knew she was right, but the subject was so huge I had been trying not to think about it.

"But where do we start?" I asked.

"Anywhere," she answered cheerfully, "just as long as we start. We're going to have to borrow money, so we'll have to convince the bank we can turn this into a profitable venture. That means having quotes for all the work and a business plan to show how it will function once it's up and running."

For a moment, I wanted to run away. It was one thing to

dream about turning a derelict classroom into an indoor play area, but quite another to draw detailed plans of what was required and come up with an accurate costing.

Mum had always handled the family's finances and kept the company accounts, but this time I knew she was going to need help.

"Okay," I said, "I guess we'd better get started."

The first step was to have a proper survey done and begin collating the quotes we needed. The list seemed endless. Fortunately, there was no problem with access to the old school, so we spent weeks going over the place with a stream of plumbers, builders, kitchen equipment suppliers, electricians, glaziers, carpet layers, decorators and others too numerous to mention.

During our frequent visits, we often called into Chudleigh to use the local shops and one day David returned with a surprised expression on his face.

"You'll never believe what I've been told," he said.

"What?" I asked.

"I was talking to the greengrocer. He used to supply all the fruit and veg when the school was open and he was keen to know if we might need stuff in the future, but then he said that he'd have to tell me straight away that he wouldn't deliver after dark."

"Why?" I asked blankly.

"You're not going to believe this. He told me he's lived in Chudleigh all his life and he's heard so many stories about Stokelake House being haunted, he won't go near it after dark."

"You're joking! Surely he was having you on?"

"No," David assured me, "he was absolutely serious."

The survey cost a small fortune but came up with nothing unexpected. The good news was the old building itself was remarkably sound. There was no sign of subsidence, dry rot, death-watch beetle or any of the other nasties we had feared.

Best of all, the damage to the roof was only superficial and replacing the missing slates would be enough to make the whole place watertight.

The modern additions, however, were another matter. Although some of the new buildings were less than fifteen years old, they were all in a poor condition and many of the flat roofs needed to be replaced.

"We'll have to do it a stage at a time," Dad said calmly, running his fingers over the plans he had spread out in front of him.

"Fortunately, most of the units in the craft block have sound roofs. We'll have to limit ourselves to those for the first year and paint over the windows of the two that leak so no one can see inside."

He drew a finger between two points on the map. "If we put a fence between here and here, we can ignore everything to the left of that line for the time being and concentrate on making a good job of the old house."

I nodded. "That makes sense. Better to come back to the rest later. After all, we're going to have enough to deal with as it is."

We planned and costed and estimated and wrote everything down in notebooks until, at last, we were ready to meet our accountant.

As we explained our plans, his expression changed from bemusement to concern. It was clear he thought we were mad.

"May I ask how many visitors you expect in your first year?"

"We're not exactly sure," I replied, "but we're hoping it will be a lot more than we're getting now."

"Naturally." He forced a smile. "And what is the anticipated spend per head?"

"Pardon?"

The accountant sighed. "Tell me, is it only a feasibility study you need, or do you require a full business plan?"

I glanced at Mum.

"We'll need both," she said firmly. "We might as well have all the help we can get when we go to see our bank manager."

"Yes," the accountant agreed. "I suspect that is exactly what you need."

~

By mid-summer, we had our paperwork together. A business plan, a feasibility study, a detailed costing, a file showing all our plans and designs, and a collection of projected incomes, expenses and profits.

We even had a name for our new venture. Silverlands. We knew Stokelake House had a lot of bad connotations locally, and we hoped a new name might signify a whole new beginning. In any case, Silverlands seemed a fitting choice for the new home of Silvers Model Circus.

With high hopes, we set out for an interview with our bank manager, Mr Wooley.

"Good morning, ladies." He welcomed us cordially and listened politely as we explained why we had come.

As Mum described our present attraction in Torquay, I pulled out the various plans and studies and laid them on the desk.

Mr Wooley reached out and picked up the papers one by one. Then he shook his head.

"I'm sorry, ladies, but I'm afraid our bank won't be able to support a venture of this sort."

"But why not?" I couldn't believe he had decided so quickly.

"I'm sorry, my dear, but it's not my decision. I would like to help you, really, I would, but bank managers these days have very little autonomy. We have to make our decisions based on bank protocol and I'm afraid this just doesn't come within our guidelines."

"But I've been a customer with this bank for thirty-five years," Mum protested. "Surely that must mean something?"

"I'm sorry."

Mr Wooley stood up to show us out. "Perhaps you'll have more luck with another bank."

"Oh, we will!" I retorted. "We're not going to give up. Silverlands will be opening next Easter. Definitely. In fact, I'll send you an invitation to the opening if you like. It's going to be amazing. We've already planned it."

"I'll look forward to it, my dear," Mr Wooley said as he closed the door behind us.

Over the next few of days, we got the same reception from every bank on the high street.

I wanted to cry with frustration, but the more we were rejected, the more determined I became to find the money from somewhere. We continued to plan every evening, working long into the night, perfecting our designs and finding ways to cut back our budgets. The figures involved still seemed frighteningly large.

One morning, Bob disappeared across to Torre Abbey to use the public telephone and came back with a strangely triumphant expression on his face.

"I've had a brainwave!" he announced.

I waited nervously. I had experienced Bob's brainwaves before.

"I remembered an old friend of mine who works for a firm of architects," Bob explained. "Ages ago he mentioned something about a merchant bank they deal with that specialises in venture capital. I don't know much about it, but

I got him to give me a phone number to get in touch with them."

"Oh," I said, wondering if I should ask what venture capital was.

"Anyway, I gave the bank a ring and asked them who was in charge. They seemed a bit surprised, but they told me the chairman is a man called James North, so I've made an appointment for you to go and see him tomorrow afternoon."

"You've what!" I couldn't believe it. Being rejected by managers was bad enough, but being laughed at by the chairman of a private bank was too much.

"You should have told us before you phoned!" I spluttered indignantly. "You had no right to…"

I looked at Mum for support, but she merely shrugged. "Think about it, Diana," she said. "What have we got to lose?"

The following afternoon I found myself sitting next to Mum in the boardroom of Torrington Merchant Bank gazing across a huge, polished wood table at the chairman.

I wore a neat grey skirt and silk blouse that I hoped gave an impression of efficient professionalism and a pair of sandals with high stiletto heels. I hadn't been sure about them, but they were the only ones I had that went with grey.

James North was a kindly but intimidating man. He was tall and stiff with a military air that made me think of a retired major and piercing blue eyes that seemed to see straight into your soul.

"Now," he said, as his secretary had supplied us with tea and a plate of iced biscuits, "what is it you want to discuss with me?"

Mum and I began our pitch at once. We had been through the story so many times, I was afraid we were beginning to sound like a double act. We explained our figures, described our plans, passed over our papers and finally ran out of things to say.

As the Mr North surveyed the papers strewn across the table, we sat back and waited for the inevitable rejection.

Finally, the banker looked up.

"Where is your current exhibition?"

I told him Silvers Model World could be found on Torquay sea front.

"Then before we discuss anything further, I had better come and see it. If you consult my secretary, she will arrange an appointment."

A few minutes later, we had arranged a visit for the following Tuesday and were standing outside in the car park.

"He didn't say no." Mum looked at me disbelievingly.

"No. He didn't, did he?" I said. "In fact, he didn't really say anything at all."

We laughed with relief all the way back to Torquay. We had been to see the chairman of a bank and he hadn't said no. For the moment, that was cause enough for celebration.

~

By Tuesday morning, we had cleaned the barn from end to end, checked all the models were working properly, changed every display in the gift shop and even swept the path leading from the seafront. We wanted everything to be perfect.

The Magic Woodland display

When Mr North arrived, I introduced everyone, then left Dad to show our visitor around the circus and the other displays. They seemed to be gone forever.

Fortunately, we had a fair number of people visiting that day, which looked impressive and also helped keep us busy. Eventually, Dad and Mr North emerged back into the gift shop and headed across to the counter where Mum and I were serving.

"I won't keep you, as you're busy," Mr North said politely. "I've seen everything I need to see. Perhaps you could make another appointment with my secretary so that we can discuss your proposals further."

I wanted to tell him I wasn't busy, that I would happily throw all the visitors out if it meant we could talk straight away, but instead, I thanked him and watched as he walked out the door.

"What did he say?" I demanded as soon as he had gone.

"Nothing much," Dad replied. "He took his time and looked at everything, but it was me that did all the talking."

"And what did you say?"

"I don't know. I just told him about the circus, about how it started, how it took over the house, how I taught you to solder in the kitchen and you melted all your mum's saucepans, that sort of thing."

"What!" I was horrified. "Dad! We're trying to look professional! You can't say things like that."

"Calm down, love." He grinned at me. "I'm only joking. All I said was that if he's got a few million pounds to spare, he should definitely give it to us."

"Oh, Dad." I flung my arms around his neck and hugged him. "I wouldn't be surprised if you did."

~

It was another three days before Mum and I were back in the boardroom of Torrington Bank. I barely slept in that time. Every night I tossed and turned, trying to guess what Mr North would say.

I didn't understand why he had said he wanted to discuss our proposals further. As far as I could see, there was nothing left to discuss. He had seen our plans, studied our figures, and visited our existing attraction. What else was there? Surely the only thing left was for him to say yes or no?

Mum hid her nerves much better than I did. To my surprise, she looked relaxed as she sipped her tea and told Mr North about our family history.

"To be honest with you," he said suddenly, "it is only because you are a family that I am considering your proposal at all. I have great faith in families. In my experience, a business run by a family that can work together has a strength and unity no other business can possess. I know that is a rather unfashionable view these days, but it is one that I stand by."

I nodded politely.

"What you are proposing is a hugely speculative venture," he continued, "but I believe that between you, you have the resolve and determination to see it through."

"We do, we do." I agreed.

"But what I have to ask myself is just how committed the family is to this enterprise. How much you are prepared to contribute towards it."

"We'll give it everything we've got," I assured him, not understanding what he meant.

"If Torrington Bank is to become involved in this project, then it will become a joint venture, a shared responsibility, if you like." He looked from one to the other of us. "And on that basis, what I am proposing is that Torrington provides half the capital sum needed, and the family provides the other half."

"But we don't have that kind of money," I protested. "That's why we need to borrow it."

"But if the bank were to put up the whole amount, the bank would be taking the whole risk," he explained patiently. "You can see that, surely. Much as we all want this project to succeed, we still have to consider what will happen if it fails. I'm afraid Torrington cannot consider contributing more than fifty percent of the capital. I suggest you consider ways of raising the rest."

"But how?" I wasn't worried about looking calm anymore. I was clutching at straws. He had offered us half a dream, but it was useless without the other half.

"What about your home?" Mr North suggested. "You could use the proceeds of a sale to provide your share of the investment. After all, a property the size of Stokelake House must have plenty of room for accommodation."

"No!" I protested. "You haven't seen the state it's in! We'll need all the decent rooms for exhibitions, the rest have got water pouring through them. And we've got two babies to think about. We can't just camp out in a derelict house. There isn't even any heating."

"Then I suggest you go back and discuss it with the others," Mr North said quietly. "I will be interested to hear what you decide."

"Do we have to go back yet?" I asked. "Couldn't we just drive around for a bit?"

"There's no point in putting it off," Mum said sadly. "It won't get any easier. Anyway, it's not fair to leave them waiting. They've been just as wound up as you have."

I knew she was right, but I was dreading having to explain the situation to the others.

Suddenly, the reality of what we were doing had crashed over me like a tidal wave. Mr North's words echoed in my head. "We have to consider what will happen if the project fails."

Bob and I had only bought our home a couple of years ago and it still had a huge mortgage on it. If we sold it, we could raise a few thousand pounds at most, but my parents' situation was different.

They had lived in the same house since they arrived in England and now, after twenty-five years of hard work, the mortgage was paid off and it belonged to them. At their age, they should have been thinking about slowing down, about spending time with their grandchildren, not risking everything they possessed on a wild dream.

The others knew something was wrong the moment we walked into the barn.

"The answer's no, then," David sighed.

"It's not as simple as that," Mum replied.

Visitors were still milling around the barn, so we had to pass on the news in hurried conversations in the ticket box and the gift shop. The others listened in silence.

The rest of the day was miserable. We smiled at the customers and did what we had to do, but as soon as the exhibition closed, we pulled a group of chairs together and sat in a dejected huddle. At least David, Phil, Bob and I did. It soon became clear that Mum and Dad had found time for a private discussion.

"It's decided," Dad said. "We're going to sell the house.

After all, it will be a lot easier to get the work done if we're living on the premises, won't it?"

"But you can't," I objected. "What if anything goes wrong? Where would you live?"

"Listen, love, with an investment as big as this, the bank is going to insist we all give personal guarantees. That means that if anything goes wrong, they'll take the house, anyway."

"But that's unfair!" I wailed.

"Don't be so negative," Mum scolded. "I thought you'd be pleased."

"I am," I said, "but what if it all goes wrong?"

"That's up to us, isn't it?" Dad said. "We have to make sure it doesn't go wrong."

"But are we seriously thinking of moving in there?" Phil asked, wide-eyed. "I mean, how will we manage?"

"There is a flat of sorts up in the attic," David said. "I don't remember exactly, but I think it has a bathroom."

"We'll have to see it as an adventure," Dad said cheerfully. "There's plenty of space, after all. We'll have to cope as best we can for the time being."

"In any case," Mum added. "It's not decided yet. Everything still depends on getting planning permission."

Once we had the finances in place, we made a formal offer for Stokelake House. It was conditional upon us getting planning permission, but we all knew there was no going back now.

A special meeting had been arranged for the planning subcommittee to hear our proposals, and Mr Turner explained that if the subcommittee supported our application, it would be formally accepted at a full planning meeting a few days later.

Everything hinged upon impressing the subcommittee.

On the appointed day, Bob and I turned up at the council offices half an hour early to get ourselves prepared. We had rehearsed our speeches until we were word perfect and had spent hours thinking of answers to questions we might be asked.

We had even made a video of our exhibitions in Torquay so we could show the quality of our displays.

"Do you have a video player we can use?" I asked Mr Turner, knowing we had a television and video player in the boot of the car, just in case.

"Yes, that's no problem. I'll show you the conference room. It's already set up for the meeting."

As we walked into the room, I stopped dead. A table stood on a dais in front of a huge semicircle of chairs.

"How many members are there on this subcommittee?" I asked.

"Thirty-eight."

"Thirty-eight?" I gasped. "Who are they?"

"Anyone who might be affected by developments on the site," Mr Turner replied.

"Such as?"

"The Planning Department, Devon County Council, Chudleigh Council, The Country Landowners Association, Chudleigh Resident's Committee, The Highways Department, The Neighbourhood Watch… shall I go on?"

I shook my head and took a deep breath. It was not a good time to panic, but my legs were trembling.

I think Bob sensed my nervousness.

"Let's get the video player set up," he suggested. "In fact, why don't we leave it running as people come in? That way, they can look at it and we might get a chance to chat to some of them before the meeting starts."

He trailed an extension lead across the dais and set the video player up on the table while I opened a box of leaflets showing how Silverlands might look once it was open.

I placed a leaflet on each chair and stood back. The video was running. Everything was ready. There was nothing to do but wait.

~

The members of the subcommittee fell into two categories. Those who were there as part of their work, such as the representatives from the Highways Department, were mainly middle-aged men wearing dark suits and carrying briefcases. The others, from associations and voluntary groups, tended to be women, and most were considerably older. No one smiled.

I have always been shy, so the thought of standing up in front of thirty-eight strangers and explaining my family's dreams and ambitions was my idea of hell.

I had planned to shake hands and introduce myself as people arrived, but my courage failed me and I stood nervously by the table on the dais with an inane smile on my lips.

Bob was far more in control of himself, and he greeted people at the door until all the chairs in the hall were filled.

Mr Turner sat in the front row and when everyone had arrived, he stood up and turned to face the others. He said a few words of welcome and briefly outlined the history of the site at Stokelake. Then he introduced Bob and me and promptly sat down again.

Thirty-eight pairs of eyes turned expectantly in our direction.

I felt sick.

Fortunately, Bob stepped forwards and beamed at everyone.

"Thank you so much for coming today," he began. "I know many of you have negative feelings about Stokelake House as a result of things that have happened in the past, but I am hoping you will listen to our proposals today with an open mind.

"As Mr Turner explained, our family has run a tourist attraction in Torquay for some years and we are hoping to move the attraction to Chudleigh. By doing this, we plan to bring new life and prosperity to a site which has had a troubled history.

"If you have had a chance to look at our leaflets, you will have an idea of the sort of exhibitions we want to include."

Bob glanced across and caught my eye. Not a single person in the audience had moved since he began speaking. It was as if we were standing in front of a collection of waxworks.

"I'm sure you all know," he ploughed on, "how important tourism is to our economy, but I would like to ask you this: Where can visitors go in this area if it rains?"

Bob waited expectantly, but there was no response.

"Exactly," he said, spreading his hands in a gesture of defeat. "You can't think of anywhere, can you? Apart from shopping centres and one or two National Trust properties, there is nowhere for holiday makers to go in bad weather.

"That is why we believe Silverlands will bring real advantages to this area. After all, there are a great many caravan parks, hotels, guest houses and self-catering apartments around here that want their visitors to have a wonderful holiday, whether the sun shines or not.

"And if we're successful and Silverlands attracts large numbers of visitors, then our success will also benefit the wider community. My wife, in particular, is keen we should promote local Devon products."

I swallowed hard and took my cue.

"Yes, I am," I said, trying to keep my voice steady. "We're going to have tearooms selling locally baked cakes and scones."

I looked around the audience, trying desperately not to make eye contact with anyone.

"And we're going to sell a wide range of local cheeses, jams, and chutneys in our gift shop."

I was acutely aware that thirty-eight pairs of eyes were now looking straight at me. There was a black mark on the wall at the back of the room. I decided to focus on it and pretend the people in front of me didn't exist.

"Another aspect of our attraction is our plan for a craft workshop," I recited. "This will provide large, spacious workshops at very reasonable rents for local craftspeople who will be able to sell their products directly to our visitors."

Suddenly I realised the dark mark on the wall was exactly the shape of a rabbit. The words froze in my throat. I was lost. I had no idea what I was supposed to say next.

"Jobs." Bob hissed at me.

"Oh, yes." I felt my cheeks flush. "Jobs… We will be creating jobs… I mean, just renovating the place is going to be a lot of work…" I trailed off as my thoughts swirled out of control.

"And once the attraction is open, we will need staff," Bob cut in. "We estimate there will be seasonal work for between six and eight local people in the first year and many more in later years as the rest of the site is brought into use."

I listened as Bob explained our plans and the benefits Silverlands would bring to the local community, but I couldn't remember a single one of the words I had rehearsed so carefully.

Finally, Bob finished and asked if anyone had any questions.

No one spoke. There was a moment's silence, then Mr Turner was back on his feet. He thanked us politely and suggested we wait outside while the subcommittee considered its recommendation.

There was a row of chairs in the corridor and I slumped down miserably.

"I'm sorry. I was useless."

Bob didn't answer, but he sat beside me and squeezed my hand.

A large, white-faced clock ticked monotonously on the wall opposite us and I listened to its rhythmic beat as I chewed my bottom lip.

It was nearly twenty minutes before Mr Turner appeared before us. There was the tiniest trace of a smile on his lips.

"You will be pleased to know that after a narrow vote, the subcommittee has decided to support your proposal."

CHAPTER 9

After that, our lives changed completely.

Within weeks, we became the proud owners of Silverlands, previously known as Stokelake House. We formed a new company with all six of us as directors and we allowed ourselves a single celebratory meal at Chudleigh's finest restaurant. Then it was down to work.

We had less than six months to transform a near-derelict building into an entertaining family attraction. We had a team of builders, plumbers and decorators standing by ready to start work, which would leave us free to devote ourselves to the displays and exhibitions.

At least, that was the plan.

In practice, every time I settled down to start designing something, there would be a shout from one end of the building or the other and I would have to drop what I was doing and rush off to see what was needed. It soon became clear that most of my work was going to be done at night once the building team had left.

Our living accommodation was far from ideal. The flat in the attic needed a lot of work, but it did at least have a bathroom and a basic kitchen. David and Phil decided they could cope there with Michael until they had time to renovate it.

At the far end of the main house was a building which had once been a carriage house. The first floor had been converted into a one-bedroom flat, and with a little work, it became an acceptable base for Mum and Dad.

There were two more flats behind the dormitory blocks, but the roof above them leaked badly and there was slime and mould on every wall. We couldn't afford the time or money it would take to make them habitable, so Bob and I decided we could make do with a few adjoining rooms and convert them into a flat later on.

There was a small bathroom immediately above the front door to the main house, so we chose that and the rooms on either side of it and moved all our possessions and Claire's toys into them. We didn't have a kitchen, but I assured Bob I would be happy living on sandwiches for a few months.

In addition to the human members of the family, we also had two large dogs to consider.

Soon after we married, Bob had arrived home one night with a hopeful expression on his face and a bedraggled young dog.

The pup had huge brown eyes, an intelligent face, and a magnificent mane of white fur.

"You don't mind if we look after him for a couple of days, do you?" Bob asked.

"No, but why? Who does he belong to?"

"I've no idea," Bob said happily, "but I think he's hungry."

As I scraped some left-over spaghetti bolognese into a bowl, Bob explained the dog had walked into our local pub and Pete, the landlord, was trying to find its owner. He had contacted the police, but in the days before microchips, they had warned him the dog shelter was overcrowded and couldn't take him.

"I think I'll call him Dino. Would you like that, boy?" The dog wagged his tail and Bob grinned. "Dino, it is then."

"And he's only staying for a couple of days until his owner turns up?" I asked.

"Of course."

I suppose I had guessed, even then, that Dino would be staying for more than a couple of days, but we were living in a comfortable house with a walled garden. Now, as our home had become three rooms in a derelict school, coping with a large dog was more of a problem.

David and Phil also had a dog that had arrived unexpectedly. Ossie was a gangly black puppy when David agreed to look after him while an old school friend went into hospital for an operation. Tragically, the operation did not go well and Ossie's owner never came home.

The awkward puppy grew into a sleek, agile dog with long silky hair and a bark like a sealion. He was the same height as Dino but much lighter built and looked much like a black, red setter.

Ossie and Dino

Fortunately, the two dogs quickly became inseparable. They loved patrolling the old house together and made friends with all the builders, plumbers and electricians we had working onsite.

The workers were a cheerful bunch and their efforts soon transformed the building. Holes were knocked through walls linking rooms together, loose plaster was removed, and rotting window frames replaced.

It was wonderful to see so much being done. Radios blared, drills screeched, and hammers thumped. There was noise everywhere, tapping, knocking and the sound of footsteps. Particularly footsteps. Even in the evenings, even at weekends, there was always the sound of footsteps.

Most of rooms were still empty and small noises echoed through the old building. I reminded myself that all old buildings creaked, but the constant noises were unsettling. When the workers left at the end of the day, I found myself checking the doors were all locked. Not an easy task when there were thirteen outside doors in the main house alone.

I wasn't the only one to notice the noises. When everyone gathered together for a cup of tea, we often heard noises that sounded like footsteps in a distant room. At first, we would rush off to find out who it was, but gradually we became accustomed to the sounds and decided to think no more about them.

The builders were unconcerned.

"Oh, that'll be Fred," one of them said as a door banged in the distance. "He'll be wanting his tea."

"Who's Fred?" I asked innocently.

"The ghost, of course. Surely you know this place is haunted?"

I smiled and went along with the joke, but I still wondered what was causing the noises.

~

We planned to transform four classrooms at the end of the main building into an indoor playground for young children. One of our most popular displays in the Spanish Barn was a feature called the Enchanted Forest, which included animated figures of the Three Little Pigs on a tandem being chased by the Big Bad Wolf on a penny-farthing.

Our plan was to extend the theme, including indoor play equipment, more models and colourful murals over the walls.

Before we could start work, however, we needed the builders to knock out some of the walls so we could open the four classrooms into a single area.

One of the decorators was a woman called Lyn, who habitually wore a long white coat, and one morning, while I was explaining to the builders exactly where I wanted the walls cut through, I saw her walk into the next room. I called to her, but she didn't stop.

Muttering to myself, I followed her into the room and stopped dead.

The room was empty.

I stared around me. There was definitely no one there.

I looked around again. There was only one door, which I had come through, and all the windows were locked.

My skin prickled as I realised what I had seen could not have been Lyn. It could not have been anyone.

I was mystified. I wanted to tell someone, but what could I say? That I had seen a ghost?

After the jokey exchanges with the builders, I knew no one would take me seriously and I couldn't blame them. I wouldn't have believed them if they had claimed to have seen a ghost either, and yet I knew I had seen something that I couldn't explain.

It dawned on me that the strangest part of the experience was that it had seemed so normal. There had been nothing about the figure that had made me think it was anything other than a living person. I tried to remember exactly what I had seen, but I wasn't sure. From the position I had been in, I should have been able to see the figure's face, and yet I had no recollection of what it had looked like.

I was completely bemused, and in the end, I decided not to say anything to anyone.

~

A few days later, I was working in the same classroom block when Mum poked her head around the door and asked if I would like a cup of tea.

"I'd love one," I replied, and as she turned to go, I saw her step into the next room.

"What about you, Lyn? I've just put the kettle on, do you..." Her voice trailed off and a moment later she was back.

"That's strange. I thought I saw Lyn," she said.

My skin prickled again.

"What did you see?"

But Mum shook her head. "It doesn't matter."

"Please tell me," I insisted. "What did you see?"

She hesitated for a moment, then closed the door and came closer to me.

"I'm not sure, but I could have sworn it was Lyn. Whoever it was, I don't understand where they went."

"What made you think it was Lyn?"

"It looked like her white coat, but I only saw her out of the corner of my eye as I was talking to you."

"And where did she go?"

"Into the next room, but there's no one there now. I must have imagined it."

"Maybe," I agreed, "but it's funny because I saw the same thing a few days ago."

Mum shot a look at me and I could see that the experience had upset her more than she was admitting.

"Really? At the time, I assumed it was Lyn, but thinking back on it, it doesn't seem quite right."

"How do you mean?"

"There wasn't any noise. I mean, you know what Lyn's like. You can always hear her coming, can't you? But there wasn't a sound. Nothing. I'm not sure it was a real person at all."

"Then what do you think it was?"

She shook her head.

"I've no idea. But it's not the only thing. I was in the kitchen the other day and the door swung shut. I told myself it must have been a breeze, but I didn't feel anything and it's such a heavy door. I usually have to push it to get it to move."

"So, do you think it could be a ghost?"

There was an expression on her face I had never seen before. It wasn't fear but rather a deep confusion and instead of answering, she simply lifted her shoulders in a shrug.

"Should we tell the others?" I asked.

She nodded. "Yes. But just with the family."

"Of course," I agreed quickly. "Just the family. The last thing we need is to have the builders laughing at us."

That evening, when the other workers had gone, Mum and I gathered everyone together.

We sat on a collection of wooden chairs in the room that would soon be our gift shop and handed around steaming mugs. The room was still as dusty and dilapidated as the rest of the building, but it had an ancient, rust-coloured carpet on the floor which gave it a homely feel compared to the bare floorboards everywhere else.

Claire and Michael were strapped into highchairs eating rusks while Mum opened a packet of biscuits. We had got into the habit of meeting up at the end of each day to compare notes on how things were going. We each had our own areas of responsibility and it gave us a chance to discuss any problems and plan ahead.

Once everyone was settled, Mum cleared her throat.

"This might sound a bit strange," she said, "but I want to ask something while we're all together."

She hesitated, and even the toddlers stopped eating and looked at her.

"I wanted to know if anyone had seen anything strange. I mean… odd. Anything that doesn't quite make sense."

"What sort of thing?" Dad asked. "Are you saying that you've seen something?"

"Well, I was probably just imagining it." Mum waved her hand dismissively as she explained what had happened earlier. "I wouldn't even have mentioned it except Diana said she's seen the same thing."

"Well, I haven't seen anything," Phil began, "but I keep hearing things. Everywhere I go I hear footsteps."

Everyone agreed. Everyone except Bob, who looked at us as if we'd gone mad.

"Let's not forget we're all tired," he reminded us. "We've been working long hours, and it's easy to start imagining things."

"Do you think we're making it up?" I challenged him.

"I didn't say that."

"Yes, you did," I persisted. "You said we were imagining things."

"Well, I didn't mean it like that. Some people get upset by the thought of ghosts, that's all. We don't want anything slowing the work down."

"Don't worry," I snapped. "I wasn't going to tell anyone else."

I knew I was being unreasonable, but Bob's reaction irritated me. In the past, I would have been sceptical too if someone had claimed to have seen a ghost, but my perspective had changed dramatically in the last few days.

And I didn't want him to think I was a hysterical woman who imagined things as soon as she got overtired. I wanted him to believe I really had seen something, but I knew there was nothing I could do to convince him. I couldn't take him back to the same spot and expect the ghost, or whatever it had been, to turn up on cue.

"Forget it," I said. "We shouldn't have brought it up."

"I didn't want to upset anyone," Mum added. "I just wanted to share what happened with the rest of you. Diana and I had already agreed it would be best not to tell anyone else."

"You haven't upset anyone..." Bob began, but I cut across him.

"No, you're right," I said sharply. "We can't afford to let anything distract us now. We need to focus. Let's just forget we even mentioned it."

"Good," Bob agreed. "I really think that would be best."

I was still feeling prickly later that day when Dad passed me in the corridor.

"Are you okay?" he asked, and I nodded unconvincingly.

"Need a chat?"

I nodded again, and Dad put an arm around my shoulder.

"Come on. It's quiet in my workshop."

Dad always had a workshop. It was impossible to imagine him without one. It would have been like imagining a tortoise without its shell. As soon as we moved into Silverlands, he had taken possession of an old science lab at the far end of the north wing and had set up his tools and machines.

Now the work surfaces were covered with lathes, vices and half-made animations he was creating for the various displays.

Dad pulled a battered tin from a shelf and offered me a custard cream.

"What's wrong?" he asked.

"I wasn't making it up, you know," I said, and he listened patiently as I repeated my story of the unexplained figure.

"But I wish I had never said anything because now everyone thinks I'm imagining things," I complained.

"I don't think you're imagining things."

Dad was the most down-to-earth person I knew, and I had been expecting him to tell me to get a grip on myself and go back to work. Instead, he offered me another biscuit.

"I didn't have a chance to say anything earlier," he explained, "but you're not the only one to have something weird happen. I haven't even mentioned it to your mum yet."

"What is it?" I asked eagerly. "What did you see?"

"I didn't see anything. That's the weird part. In fact, it was all so peculiar I decided I'd better keep it to myself. I thought if I told anyone, they'd think I'd gone nuts. The thing is, on the day we moved in, I went to the loos at the back of the house. I was standing there, doing my business at the urinals, when I heard this woman's voice right behind me."

He grinned. "I can tell you, I've never zipped up so fast in my life! I turned around like lightning, but there was no one there. Can you believe it? I looked in the corridor, but there was no one there either. I even hollered out. I was standing there, shouting 'Hello? Who is it?'"

He chuckled at the memory.

"But afterwards I couldn't remember what she'd said. Just that it had been a posh voice. Very polite and cultured. A real lady's voice. Not the sort of accent you usually hear in a gents' loo."

I laughed and Dad chuckled again as he continued.

"The worst thing is, I've been working at that end of the house all week and now I have to walk right to the other end of the site if I need to go."

"You mean you're afraid to go back in the loo?"

"No, not afraid, but it's hard to get in the mood when you

think there might be a posh lady looking over your shoulder."

"Are you going to tell anyone?"

"Well, I might tell your Mum, but I think Bob's right. It's better kept to ourselves for now. I don't believe in ghosts, but I can't give you a sensible explanation either. Come here."

He gave me an enormous hug.

"Remember, if you have any problems with ghosts-in-white-coats just send them to me. I'll sort them out for you."

CHAPTER 10

At the beginning of November, Bob came back from a trip to Exeter bouncing with excitement.

"I've got a potter!" he announced as though he had caught a prize fish. "A really good potter. He's won awards and everything."

"That's fantastic!" I smiled. Work was due to start on the craft block and I was delighted that we already had our first craftsperson lined up.

"There's just one tiny issue."

Something in Bob's voice worried me.

"What's that?"

"Nothing serious. It's just that he needs to move in straight away."

"But that's impossible!"

Bob waved aside my protests.

"Don't worry. The room at the far end will be OK. The roof isn't leaking and if we replace the broken window, it will be quite secure. He says he won't mind the work going on around him."

"But why can't he wait?"

"It's a bit complicated. There's a problem with his current

landlord and he needs to move out straight away. It's lucky for us, really, because he's going to be perfect. How great will it be for the public to watch him making things on a potter's wheel? And once he's here, I bet we'll get other craftspeople queuing up to get in."

I wasn't convinced, but it was hard to discourage Bob once he had made up his mind.

"When does he want to come?"

"Not until tomorrow," Bob replied airily. "He has to arrange the transport first."

~

The following day, I was in the kitchen discussing how the new catering equipment was going to be fitted when I heard the sound of a large lorry driving up from the gate.

Hurrying out through the kitchen yard, I was surprised to see a tall, thin figure in corduroy trousers, a leather jacket and a tartan cap walking backwards and giving directions to the lorry driver as the vehicle rolled along the narrow driveway towards the craft block.

"Hello!" I called out. "Can I help you?"

"No," the man in the cap replied without looking in my direction.

"Excuse me," I tried again, "what are you doing?"

"I would have thought it was clear enough." I guessed he was in his early sixties and he sounded impatient. "I'm delivering my kiln and I don't have much time. I need to get it in before dark."

"Oh, I see. You must be the potter."

The man shot me a disapproving glance. "Yes, that's me," he growled. "The Potter. No name required."

"I'm sorry. My husband didn't mention your name."

"Of course not. Why would he?"

"Well, I'm very pleased to meet you. I'm Diana. What is your name, by the way?"

"I'm Tom Stevens. Tom the Potter. Or just The Potter. Whichever."

"Oh. Well, I will call you Tom, if that's all right?"

There was no reply, and after a moment, I decided to retreat.

"In that case, I'll tell Bob you've arrived."

An hour later, I heard Bob's voice echoing from the craft block and couldn't control my curiosity. I hurried across and was astounded to see the lorry parked squarely across the path and backed right up to the wall of the building.

There were pieces of glass and splintered wood scattered across the ground, and for a moment, I thought there had been an accident. As I got closer, I realised the entire window, including the frame, had been removed and what was left of it was leaning against the wall.

The lorry was the type used to deliver palettes of bricks and had a large hydraulic hoist on the back. Below it, swinging gently on long chains, was a square metal object that I guessed was the kiln. It was enormous.

I could see Tom the Potter's corduroy cap bobbing around inside the building and Bob, looking worried, talking to the lorry driver.

"How's it going?" I asked, and Bob frowned.

"Not well. The kiln's much bigger than I'd expected, and it's lined with special bricks so it weighs a ton. There's no way it could go through the door. We've had to take the window out, but the driver's worried because every time he tries to manoeuvre it, the kiln stays to sway."

"Oh, dear."

I didn't know what else to say.

"I'm going to give it another go." The driver's voice came from inside the cab.

"Okay," Bob shouted back.

There was a deep roar as the winch ground into action and the arm of the hoist moved towards the gap where the window had been.

Suddenly, the kiln juddered and the chains holding it grated alarmingly. It swung towards the building and the pitch of the winch dropped as the driver tried to steady the movement, but instead of slowing, the kiln jerked towards the wall.

The driver swore above the scream of the engine as he struggled to regain control. The winch arm lifted, and for a moment, I thought the kiln would stop, but instead, it crunched against the wall and lumps of plaster and shards of concrete block flew everywhere.

I ducked as a cloud of gritty dust showered over me. Blinking away tears and coughing violently, I shook debris from my hair as the Potter's angry face appeared at the window.

"For Christ's sake!" he bellowed. "I thought you knew what you were doing!"

The driver threw open the cab door and climbed out.

"Look, mate," he growled as he surveyed the damage, "I'm only doing this as a favour, remember? You told me it would be an easy job. You never said anything about having to put the damned thing through a bloody window!"

"Through a door, through a window, what's the difference?" the Potter exploded. "Just not through the wall! Have you any idea how much that kiln is worth?"

"Let's all calm down, shall we?" Bob suggested. "What matters now is how we're going to resolve this..."

"Not my problem, mate." The driver turned on him. "I'm dropping this damned thing right here and you two can work out what the hell you're going to do with it."

"You can't do that!" the Potter roared.

"Just watch me!"

"Please! Let's not be hasty!" Bob hurried after the driver as he climbed back into his cab. "Maybe we can come to an arrangement..."

That evening, Bob and I sat in silence as we ate our meal. Claire was asleep in the next room and we were both exhausted. It had taken Bob ages to persuade the driver to have one more attempt at lifting the kiln and it had taken me as long to persuade the Potter to keep quiet until it was done.

Eventually, we had tied ropes to the corners of the kiln and Bob, David, Dad and Tom had pulled on the ropes so the kiln couldn't swing while it was being moved.

Four concrete blocks had been placed on the floor of the unit to ensure the kiln would have air passing underneath it and it had been my job to give directions so the kiln could be lowered exactly into place.

Unfortunately, because it had taken so long to calm the situation, the cold winter's afternoon had given way to a dark moonless night. The electricity supply to the craft block had not yet been connected, so the whole operation had to be carried out by torchlight.

However, after several attempts and a lot of careful manipulation, the kiln had finally been settled into place and the Potter was satisfied.

We had left him hammering a sheet of plywood across the gaping window and returned gratefully to the main building.

Now, as we looked back on the day's events, we saw the funny side of the situation.

"Well, it wasn't the afternoon I had planned," Bob admitted as he leaned back in his chair.

"I know, but it could have been worse. At one point, I thought they were going to bring the whole wall down."

"Yes." Bob grinned. "I've never seen anyone attack a wall with a kiln on a chain before."

"It reminded me of one of those demolition balls they use for taking down old buildings. Maybe we could borrow it. We still have a lot more holes in walls to make ourselves."

"You're right," Bob laughed, "but I'll let you ask the Potter!"

The following day, when I went to check on the builders, one of them showed me something he had found tucked away behind a skirting board. It was a large, straight-bladed knife.

I turned it over in my hands and a coating of rust stained my fingers.

"How on earth could that have got down there?" I asked.

"It must have been hidden," the builder replied. "This place had a pretty tough reputation, you know."

I had heard that Stokelake House had been a school for difficult children, but until then, I hadn't thought about what that meant.

"But this could be lethal," I said, looking at the pointed blade.

"And look here—" the builder jabbed a finger at two small notches carved into the handle.

I looked at him blankly.

"It's an old gangster thing," he explained. "It used to be in all the old movies. Each time they used a knife to attack someone, they carved a notch in it."

"And you think one of the boys at the school hid it down there?"

"I can't think of any other explanation, can you?"

I handed the knife back to him.

"I think you'd better get rid of it."

Later that day, as the family gathered for yet another cup of tea, I mentioned the knife.

"This must have been a pretty grim school," I said. "It hadn't occurred to me before, but the holes in the corridor walls look as though they've been kicked in."

"Yes," David agreed, "and have you noticed how many of the downstairs windows have bars on them? Do you think they were to keep people out or to keep people in?"

"And have you seen the windows in the shower block?" Dad asked.

We all shook our heads.

"Have a look next time you pass. The ones on the bottom corridor. The windows have bars on them, but they've never had any glass in them."

"You're joking?" I was horrified. "I noticed there was no glass, but I just thought it was missing."

"No." Dad shook his head. "The bars have been fitted right through the frames, so there's no way you could put glass in them. Those showers must have been absolutely freezing."

"And they had an armoury," David added unexpectedly.

"A what?" Phil asked.

"An armoury, for keeping guns. It's down in the basement. The steel cabinets are still screwed to the wall and there's a piece of card stuck inside one of them with a list of the guns that were kept in it."

"I'm beginning to understand why the locals didn't like the place," Mum said.

"You're not suggesting the guns were for the teachers?" Phil asked.

"No, I think it was more of a cadet thing," David said.

"Maybe it was like a boot camp, and they were really into army training and discipline?"

"Well, whatever it was, Stokelake School is in the past," Mum said firmly. "None of it matters anymore. We have to concentrate on the future and how we are going to turn this place into a happy family attraction."

~

Work progressed quickly and, by the end of November, the new roofs were on the craft block and the units were drying out. Some of the walls needed to be re-plastered and there were sections of floor that would have to be replaced, but it was easy to imagine the rooms filled with artists, craftspeople, and a cheerful buzz of activity.

At the beginning of December, Bob had a phone call from a woodcarver called Dougal.

Like Tom the Potter, Dougal needed to move urgently and offered to complete the work on his unit himself if he could move straight in.

I suppose we all have stereotypes in our minds. I had never met a woodcarver before, and looking back, I think I had expected him to be like the woodchopper from Little Red Riding Hood, tall, muscular and tanned.

I was surprised to find Dougal was tiny, far shorter than myself, with delicate white skin, an explosion of grey hair and a soft Celtic voice that was so quiet I struggled to catch his words.

He told me he had been particularly keen to rent a unit because the craft block was positioned at the junction of three ley lines.

I had no idea what he was talking about. I had never heard of ley lines and did not know what they signified.

I soon learned that Dougal was an expert on everything psychic or spiritual. He held a cleansing ceremony before he moved into the unit, wafting aromatic smoke from an ornate brass container while humming quietly to himself.

Later, he showed me a map of Devon with a multitude of wavy blue lines drawn across it and told me they represented ley lines. Sensing my confusion, he explained that, just as electricity moves around the country through a grid of physical cables, so psychic power moves along ley lines and people who understand the secrets of the spiritual world can access psychic strength by tapping into them.

For a moment, I thought he was teasing me, but the sincere expression in his eyes convinced me he was in earnest. When he offered to cleanse my aura for me, I made an excuse and hurried back to the main house.

To be honest, none of us were sure what to make of Dougal.

He showed Bob a photo of a beautiful oak tree and asked if he could see the spirits hiding in the branches. Bob studied it carefully but couldn't make out anything except leaves.

Dougal looked disappointed, but he explained that not everyone had his gift. He spoke to David about auras and spirit guides, and for once, David was lost for words.

But whatever his beliefs might have been, there was no denying Dougal's woodwork was amazing.

He created the most beautiful objects and instinctively knew how to use the grain and formations within the wood to their best advantage. We had no doubt his work would be very popular with the public and were confident Dougal and Tom the Potter would be the start of a happy community of craftspeople.

It was only when I discovered Tom the Potter was a regular member of his church choir and had a deep dislike of anything New Age, that I began to have doubts.

Phil heard raised voices coming from the craft block, and Tom started to drop into the main house each morning, protesting about Dougal's activities.

Tom told us Dougal had taken to leaving incense sticks burning overnight, and he wanted us to ban them as a fire risk. He also wanted us to ban Dougal from playing "white noise" while he was meditating, as Tom was sure it was triggering his migraines.

When I spoke to Dougal, he counterattacked with his own complaints, telling me Tom had started cooking kippers every lunchtime because he had heard Dougal was allergic to fish.

"It's like dealing with children," I muttered when I told Dad what was happening. "I don't know how to handle them."

"If they're behaving like children, treat them like children," Dad said simply. "Tell them if they can't play nicely, you will take their toys away and make them sit on the naughty step."

"I only wish it was that easy," I sighed.

The complaints continued, and I did my best to keep the peace, but shortly before Christmas, Tom burst into my office without even knocking on the door.

"He's gone too far this time!" he shouted. "You have to make him leave."

"Whatever's the matter?" I asked.

"You should never have let that heathen take a unit," Tom snapped. "Haven't you worked it out yet? The man's a Satanist!"

"A Satanist?"

"You heard me. He's performing a ritual in his unit at this very moment."

"A ritual?"

"Yes! Stop repeating what I say and come and stop him."

"Me? But..." I was about to call for Bob when Tom grabbed my arm and tugged me towards the door.

"Quick. There's no time to waste."

As we approached the craft block, I caught the scent of

something cooking. Or burning. I wasn't sure which. Opening the door to Dougal's unit, I was greeted by the sight of a table covered in blood and feathers.

"You see!" Tom said triumphantly. "He's making a sacrifice."

Dougal looked up innocently, his hands covered in blood.

"Good morning, Diana. How are you today?"

I hesitated, completely at a loss. The smell of cooking was strong and as I looked around, I saw a small camping stove with a frying pan of meat on top of it. Sitting beside the stove, wagging its tail, was a small terrier.

"You haven't met Beelzebub yet, have you?" Dougal smiled.

"Dear God!" Tom erupted behind me.

"Dougal, what, exactly, are you doing?"

"Oh, this…" he looked down as if seeing the bloody mess for the first time. "I'm cooking Bee some breakfast. There was a dead pheasant by the side of the road earlier, and it seemed such a waste to leave it. It's perfectly fresh."

I tried to think of something sensible to say but failed.

There was a long pause, then Tom the Potter marched across the room and the door slammed shut.

"Don't mind him," Dougal said as he turned back to the pheasant. "He's a bit of a strange one, isn't he?"

"Is your dog really called Beelzebub?" I asked.

"No. Her name's Beatrice, or Bee for short, but I'm thinking of changing it."

His voice was expressionless, but as he looked at me, I saw there was a twinkle in his eyes.

"I thought I might make a little kennel for her with BEELZEBUB LIVES HERE in big gothic letters. It could go outside the door to my unit."

"No, Dougal," I pleaded. "Just… No."

Christmas was rather restrained that year.

We had committed every penny we possessed to achieving our dream and had taken on a considerable amount of debt. We had no money left for non-essentials, but fortunately, the children were too young to want expensive presents and the rest of us were grateful to take a couple of days off and relax.

Bob's three big daughters all came to visit, and we proudly showed them how the work was progressing.

~

As soon as Christmas was over, we returned to work with renewed enthusiasm. We could hardly believe that in less than four months, our attraction would be open to the public.

Most of the structural repair work had been done and now we moved on to creating the various displays we had planned.

The outside of the building still needed to be rendered and painted, but the builders had advised us to wait until the weather was warmer as render did not set well in the cold. Obviously, this meant the outside painting and decorating would have to wait, but we weren't worried as we had plenty to keep us busy.

David was the sociable one of the family and had a habit of making friends wherever he went. If he needed to go into Chudleigh to the local shops, you could be sure that by the time he returned he would not only be on first-name terms with the shopkeepers, but would know their entire life histories.

Sometimes, this was useful, and he uncovered lots of interesting stories about the history of Stokelake House.

We learned the family who had first built the house had been wealthy landowners, but the father had died shortly before the outbreak of the First World War and his son had enlisted in the army to fight for King and Country.

Sadly, the son had been killed in France and soon afterwards, the family had been hit by a double demand for inheritance tax.

Struggling to keep the estate intact, the bereaved mother and daughter had decided to open their home as a school.

For nearly fifty years, Stokelake School had been a refined establishment for young ladies from good families.

I can remember David showing us a collection of black and white photos he had been given of girls in demure, ankle-length dresses, standing in neat rows on the front lawn.

The faded images gave us a glimpse into a forgotten world and we were so inspired by them we decided to put together an exhibition showing what life had been like when Stokelake House was first built.

We found some intriguing examples of innovative Victorian technology, including a hand-pumped vacuum cleaner and a radio the size of a small fridge. There was also a working wind-up gramophone, complete with wax cylinders that played popular songs from the music halls.

I couldn't resist playing the gramophone occasionally while I was working on the exhibitions, and the scratchy sound of the old recordings always made me smile. I found myself thinking about the different people who had lived in the house over the years and wondering if they had loved it as much as I did.

From the moment I stepped into the old building, I had felt at peace and now, after only a few months of living and working there, I couldn't imagine myself being anywhere else.

Silverlands was my home, but it was also my mission. I wanted to turn it into something truly special. I wanted it to be a place where families could be happy and reconnect with each other. Somewhere people could forget their problems and spend time laughing and relaxing.

It had seemed an impossible dream at first, but now I really believed we could transform the neglected wreck we had discovered into a wonderful family attraction.

It worried me we only had a few months left to get everything finished, but we had overcome so many obstacles already that I was confident we would succeed. The building work was progressing, and the exhibitions were taking shape. We had brought our most popular displays from the Spanish Barn and planned to expand on them. In addition, we were going to create several completely new attractions.

At the far end of the house, above the Enchanted Forest play area, was another block of four classrooms. These were going to be transformed into a display called Devon Mysteries, devoted to local folklore and ghost stories.

Outside, Philippa had been busy supervising work on the Animal Meadow and the fencing and stables were well under way. We already had a few animals in residence, including a miniature bullock and four adorable goats.

Phil and David with our goats, Ted and Angus.

Yes, everything was going well as we reached the middle of January. I can remember smiling as I spotted snowflakes drifting down outside the bedroom window. It had been several years since we had seen snow in Devon and, even then, it had been restricted to a few short-lived flurries on the hilltops and the moors.

I was sure the children would be excited to have their first glimpse of snow and I hurried Claire to the window to make sure she had a chance to see the beautifully fragile flakes before they stopped.

But the snow didn't stop. The huge fluttering snowflakes kept drifting down, and within twenty-four hours, not only Devon but the whole of the country was buried beneath a white blanket.

We had all been so preoccupied with our plans that none of us had been watching the weather forecasts and we were taken completely by surprise.

We were not the only ones. Across the country, trains stopped running, motorways were blocked by stranded vehicles, schools were closed, hospitals and essential services struggled to cope and everything came to a standstill.

The constant hum of traffic on the A38 faded to a low rumble and several of our builders phoned in saying they would not be able to come to work as they lived along country lanes, which were impassable.

At first it was exciting. There is something wonderfully tranquil about gently falling snow, and the clean, sparkling expanse of white lawns made Stokelake House look magical.

We took Claire and Michael outside, bundled up in their winter clothes, and they toddled about happily, crunching the strange white carpet beneath their feet. The dogs barked, begging for sticks to be thrown, or chased each other wildly, sending white flurries shooting into the sky.

Even the goats seemed excited by the new conditions. They were still only half grown and careered around their field, full of boisterous energy.

Philippa was less amused, however, when she discovered all the outside taps were frozen solid, which meant carrying buckets of water up the hill from the main house.

That evening we watched the news and were shocked to see the disruption across the country. In some areas, the snow was already several feet deep, and it was expected to get worse.

We looked at each other uneasily and wondered what effect this was going to have on our tight schedules. We could afford to lose a few days, but after that we would be getting into dangerous territory.

When the news ended, the weather forecast gave no indication of how long the arctic conditions were likely to last.

"There's no point in worrying about it," Dad said practically. "There's still plenty we can get on with. If needs be, we will have to ask the builders if they can work a few weekends to catch up once this is all over."

The following morning, the snow was still falling as Philippa carried buckets of water uphill through the deepening drifts. To her surprise, Tom the Potter appeared beside her and offered to carry a bucket.

"You're here early," she said.

"Not really," Tom sighed. "I didn't go home last night. My car doesn't like hills in the summer. There's no way it would make it up and down Haldon Hill in this weather. I need to get my stock built up ready for the summer, so I can't afford to get stranded at home."

"You mean you slept in the craft block?" Phil asked. "You must be frozen."

"Not at all," Tom replied dismissively. "I have some blankets I use for the kiln while it's cooling, and those were perfectly adequate."

"But what about food? You can't walk into Chudleigh in this. I've been watching people across the valley and they can't even get up the hill with four-wheel drives."

"Yes, that is more of a problem," Tom agreed.

Soon the distant noises of vehicles slithering and sliding along the A38 ceased altogether, and an eerie silence took their place.

We were not surprised when none of our builders turned up for work.

Chudleigh was barely a mile away, but it was on the other side of a deep valley. For the time being, reaching it either by vehicle or on foot was simply not possible. From the house we could see abandoned vehicles half-buried in the snow and we learned from news reports that even snow ploughs had become stranded in places.

We were cut off.

Fortunately, we were well supplied with food, so we decided to keep working as best we could until everything returned to normal.

A new central heating system had been installed through the old house with radiators fitted everywhere, but unfortunately, the boiler had not yet been connected.

We had brought a handful of electric fires with us when we moved in, but they made little impact in the enormous old building. The two most powerful fires were reserved for the children's bedrooms and the rest were gathered together in the soon-to-be gift shop.

Even with a fire in each corner, the room was far from warm, but it gave us somewhere to thaw out over a cup of tea.

We reminded each other that snow never lasted long in Devon, and until the thaw arrived, we would have to cope by putting on extra jumpers.

Philippa had told me Tom the Potter was stranded in the craft block, so I invited him to join us for meals. He did not look thrilled by the idea, but arrived bundled up in layer upon layer of clothes with a brightly coloured knitted hat pulled down over his ears.

Claire eyed him warily.

"I shall have to repay you," Tom announced as he ate his meal.

"There's no need for that," Bob answered quickly. "We couldn't leave you to starve, could we?"

"I insist. I will work for my supper. I can spare a few hours, so I will report for work in the morning."

"Okay, that would be great."

As soon as the meal was over, Tom stood up and headed for the door.

"Thank you, and good evening," he said. "I will be back first thing tomorrow morning for instructions."

"He's a bit of an individual, isn't he?" Mum remarked later when we told the others about Tom's offer.

"Eccentric. That's the word for him," David agreed.

"It's kind of him to help but what can we get a potter to do?" Philippa asked.

We looked at each other uncertainly.

"Painting," Dad suggested. "The red corridor's ready to be done. The builders have finished all the repairs there and the paint's in the storeroom."

"Perfect. That should keep him busy."

Stokelake House had originally consisted of two sections. The first was the main house itself, which had elegant architecture, beautiful ceilings, a wide, sweeping staircase, and huge bay windows.

The second section, which adjoined the main house, had once been a U-shaped complex with a coach house at the back flanked by two stable blocks with a courtyard in the middle.

The front part of the U-shape had long been filled in with a double-storied classroom block, leaving only a small, internal courtyard between the new block and the original coach house.

Upstairs, a narrow corridor ran the length of the old coach house, linking the main house with the area that would soon become our Devon Mysteries exhibition. For some reason, the floor had been painted a deep crimson, so inevitably, it became known as the Red Corridor.

Tall windows, which ran the length of the corridor, looked down into the courtyard and made it a bright, cheerful place. The reflected light from the snow outside made it even brighter as I showed Tom what we wanted him to do.

"You want me to paint a wall?" he asked in a flat tone.

"If you don't mind." I felt I had insulted him. "It would really help because we're getting a bit behind schedule."

He sniffed.

"If that's what you want. For the next two hours, I am at your disposal."

~

An hour later, I took up a cup of coffee. Tom didn't drink tea, or at least not the type that we had available, and I was impressed to find he had already finished over half of the corridor.

"That looks great!" I said brightly.

Tom was perched on top of a stepladder and came down when he saw the steaming mug I held out to him.

"It's not covering well," he complained. "I have to keep going back over the same area to get a decent finish."

"Never mind, you're going really quickly." I smiled. "Do you want a biscuit?"

"Thank you," he said, taking a bourbon. "Yes, I should be able to finish this today."

I was working in the kitchen when Tom tapped me on the shoulder, making me jump.

"You have a problem."

"What sort of a problem?"

"Follow me," he said and turned on his heel.

Obediently, I trotted behind him up to the red corridor and gasped in horror.

The floor was no longer red. The paint Tom had rollered across the walls was now spreading in puddles across the floor.

"What happened?"

"It must be the cold," Tom explained. "The paint isn't drying. It's slipping."

I looked more carefully and saw the bottom half of the wall was still coated with glistening colour, but the top half had only a thin film over it. The paint was literally sliding down onto the floor.

"I don't believe it! What can we do?"

The Potter's face was expressionless.

"Not much, I suspect. You could try scraping the paint off the floor and reapplying it to the walls, but I suspect it would be a futile exercise."

His calm voice infuriated me.

"But we have to do something!" I wailed. "That's a whole tin of paint wasted apart from anything else."

"If you use a scraper, you can probably get a lot of it back in the tin. I'll be off now. See you again tomorrow."

I had an urge to grab the tin and empty what was left of the paint over his head, but I controlled myself and waited until he had gone before screaming out loud in frustration.

CHAPTER 11

"He has to be the most annoying man on the planet!" I moaned to Dad. "I had to clean the whole corridor."

"It wasn't his fault the paint didn't dry."

"That's not the point!" I spluttered indignantly. "He could at least have looked upset. If I'd made a mess like that, I would have died of embarrassment, but he just walked off and left me to it. And now I'll have to think of something else for him to do tomorrow."

"That's easy." Dad grinned. "Get him to help you with the water."

"Oohh, yes," I smiled. "Good thinking."

We were all taking turns carrying buckets of water up to the animals and the next morning, I enlisted Tom to help me. By now, the wind had blown the snow into drifts that were far deeper than our wellie boots, and the inevitable result was wet socks and frozen feet.

It was a long, slippery slog up the hill to the stables with a heavy bucket in each hand, and I was looking forward to being back inside when I noticed a figure picking its way across the meadow towards us. I knew there were other houses along the valley, but we had not yet had a chance to meet any of our neighbours.

As the figure approached, I saw it was an elderly man with a shotgun over his arm.

"Hello!" I shouted out as he came towards us. "Lovely day, isn't it?"

"What the hell do you think you're playing at?" The man's voice thundered back at me. "You can't go around cutting off people's water!"

I stared at him.

"You are the people that bought Stokelake House, aren't you?" the man demanded.

"Yes," I answered warily.

"Then you'd better turn it back on this minute!"

"Excuse me, sir, but what water are you talking about?" Tom asked politely.

"You know very well!" the man roared, his face turning crimson with anger. "You've cut off our water supply and I'm not going to stand for it!"

As he came closer, the gun bounced on his arm and my stomach tensed.

"Why would we cut off your water?" I asked, putting down the buckets I was carrying. "We don't even know who you are."

The man ignored me and looked towards Tom.

"The name's Darwin, and if you think you can mess with me, you'll find you're wrong. I'm a JP. A Justice of the Peace. Live at the Manor House along the valley."

"But why do you think we've cut off your water?" I repeated.

"Our water comes across your land." The old man was only feet away from us now. "Always has done. Since before my time. Well, it stopped this morning, and it has to be reinstated. Immediately."

"But why do you think it has anything to do with us?" I

persisted.

Finally, he turned and glared at me, but his words were still addressed to Tom.

"You'd better explain to your daughter, here, how things are." He shifted the shotgun clumsily and the steel barrel glinted in the morning light. "We don't take kindly to being messed with in these parts."

Tom stepped forward, placing himself between me and the old man. "This is not my daughter, actually she's...."

"I don't care who she is!" Mr Darwin barked. "I want this resolved now."

"Look, sir." Tom's tone was soothing. "There's clearly a misunderstanding. It's been below freezing for days. Perhaps your pipes have frozen."

"Nonsense! They've never frozen before. Never. And it's not just us. None of the others have water, either."

"Others?" I peered around Tom's arm.

"The other properties along the valley," Mr Darwin snapped. "Eight of them, I think, including the farm."

"And their water comes through here, too?" I asked.

"Where else would it come from?"

His voice was rose dangerously, and the gun bobbed up and down.

"It's no good denying it!" Mr Darwin bellowed. "I've spoken to my son. He's a solicitor."

He lifted the gun higher on his arm and the black holes at the barrel ends were huge and threatening.

"Why don't we go inside and discuss this over a cup of tea?" Tom suggested.

"Tea?" Mr Darwin spluttered. "Foul stuff. Never touch it!"

The gun jerked again, and something inside me snapped.

"For Christ's sake!" I shouted, stepping out from behind Tom. "Nobody here has cut your water supply. Even if we had, waving a gun at us isn't going to solve anything!"

The old man looked at the gun in surprise.

"Wasn't waving it," he muttered. "Always carry it. Good weather for foxes. Stand out like bloody pumpkins against all this snow."

"Well, it feels as if you're waving it…" I said lamely.

There was a moment's silence, then Mr Darwin let the gun drop to his side before jabbing a finger at me.

"If you don't reinstate our water by tomorrow, I'll have the police out to arrest you."

Lost for words, I could only glare back at him.

"You have until noon," he said dramatically before turning and crunching his way back across the meadow.

Tom watched him go.

"What a delightful man. I pity any poor criminal that comes up before him on the bench."

"I'd like to see him get the police out here at the moment," David said as we explained what had happened. "I don't think their police cars are equipped with four-wheel drive, so they're just as stuck as everyone else."

"I'm still not sure if he was drunk or just demented," I said. "He was probably talking a load of rubbish, but he was quite certain that his water supply runs across our land."

"Maybe it does," Bob said, "but I don't remember anything being said about it. Shouldn't the solicitors have told us if there was something like that?"

"I can get the paperwork out if you like," Mum offered. "I don't remember reading anything about water supplies in the deeds or the searches, but I may have missed something."

I phoned our solicitor, but he didn't seem unduly concerned.

"I wouldn't worry too much about it," he said. "Services are often a problem with old estates. The water and electrical supplies are sometimes left off the plans. They were probably installed when the house was built and at that time the other properties may well have been part of the estate, so it's quite conceivable that they would be on your supply."

"But what are we supposed to do?" I asked. "He's insisting that it's up to us to reinstate his supply. Surely it's his problem if anything's gone wrong with his pipes?"

The solicitor hesitated.

"Actually, it's a bit of a grey area. If there is a historic right to a water supply across your land, then technically, it would be your responsibility to maintain the pipes."

"You mean we will have to pay to repair his pipes?"

"Er, yes. I'm afraid so."

"But we don't even know where they are."

"No. I can see that might be a problem."

I put the phone down and wondered how much this was going to cost.

The rest of the family was outraged when I told them what the solicitor had said.

"That's ridiculous!" David objected. "How can it be our responsibility? I thought solicitors were supposed to do searches for things like that? We ought to sue his company for negligence."

"Maybe you're right," I agreed, "but it won't help us right now. This Darwin man is going to be turning up at any minute, wanting to know what we're going to do about his water supply."

"It doesn't matter how much he rants, there's nothing anyone can do until the weather improves." Mum sighed.

"The first thing is to calm him down while we decide what to do," Dad said. "One of the properties is a farm, isn't it? They must have a tractor or something that can cope with the snow. Maybe they can arrange to distribute water to the other properties if we let them fill up here."

"Good plan," David said. "But if he turns up with a gun again, I still think we should get him arrested."

It was exactly noon when Mr Darwin banged on the front door. He was unarmed, so I invited him in and introduced him politely to Bob.

I tried to offer him a drink, but he dismissed me with a brusque shake of his hand.

He listened impatiently as Bob pointed out that nothing could be done while the freezing weather persisted, but brightened up when he heard our plan.

"That's more like it," he grunted. "I knew you'd see sense. Only a short-term arrangement, mind you. As soon as the thaw arrives, I expect the supply to be reinstated properly or I will instruct my solicitors."

"Of course, I don't doubt that for a moment," Bob said sweetly.

Mr Darwin frowned at him, screwing his eyes into tight little spots, then turned on his heel and marched out of the house.

Later that day, we heard a rumble of traffic.

Racing to an upstairs window, I saw that, in the distance, a few vehicles were moving on the dual carriageway.

We celebrated over a cup of tea and went back to work, but it was another two days before snow ploughs cleared the last of the sideroads and our builders were able to return.

It was a huge relief to see work start again, but the conditions were still challenging and progress was slowed by the problems of working in freezing conditions. Even indoors, buckets of water quickly froze over, and it was simply impossible to work with plaster or paint.

Everything took much longer than it should have done.

We spent hours each day carrying food and water for the animals and deliveries we needed were delayed as the country struggled to get back to normal.

As we slipped further and further behind schedule, I began to panic. The others were concerned too, so we pored over our plans, looking for corners to cut.

I knew things would be easier if only we could get the heating system working, but it seemed every plumber in Devon was out dealing with emergencies caused by the extreme weather.

There was nothing we could do but carry on as best we could.

~

It was February before the new boiler was finally in operation and a delicious warmth pumped around the house.

We had less than two months left until Silverlands was due to open and we were weeks behind schedule.

I had been certain that once the temperature rose, our work rate would increase, but I should have known the thaw would bring problems of its own.

Phil had been eagerly looking forward to using the standpipe in the Animal Meadow again, but one morning she was shocked to find the path leading to the entrance had become a stream. It seemed the freeze had blown the joints of the water pipes supplying the stables, and now the pipes had thawed, water bubbled up through the ground and flowed freely down the hillside.

After several phone calls, we found a plumber who said he could come out the following day.

"Why can't he come out now?" Phil demanded.

"He's already dealing with an emergency," Bob replied.

"But this is an emergency too!" Phil wailed. "The water's washing away the new flowerbeds, and the goat pen is a lake. If it gets any deeper, it's going to flood the food store."

"There must be a stopcock," Dad said. "We need to cut the supply until the plumber can get here. Does anyone know where it is?"

We all shook our heads.

"What about the builders? They might know," David suggested.

They didn't.

I scanned all the ground plans we had been given, but there was nothing.

Going back to the field, I found Tom the Potter helping Phil dig a trench to divert the muddy water away from the stables.

"I preferred the snow." Tom sighed as I passed. "Far more aesthetically pleasing."

In the distance, I spotted David walking across the top field, prodding the ground with a stick.

"What are you doing?" I called.

"Trying to find this bloody stopcock," he shouted back. "The builders think it's somewhere around here."

"Wonderful."

Much of the field was still covered by dirty clumps of melting snow and the rest was an ankle-deep tangle of grass and weeds.

"How are we supposed to find it?" I called as I hurried across.

"No idea. Just keep looking, I suppose. What else can we do?"

"But we could waste days walking around here and still not find it," I objected. "Shouldn't we get on with the exhibitions?"

"Any luck?" Tom the Potter asked as David and I walked back down the hill.

I shook my head, and Tom must have read my mood.

"If you're desperate, you could try the Warlock," he said.

"The what?"

"Dougal. If you believe his claims, he can divine anything."

"How does that work?" I asked.

"I would prefer not to know," Tom said haughtily. "He's probably a charlatan, of course, so don't offer to pay him whatever you do, but he claims he can find anything underground from lost wedding rings to mineral deposits."

"That's not possible, is it?"

"Of course not," Tom agreed cheerfully. "It's a load of bunkum, but if you're really desperate, what have you got to lose?"

"Is he in today?"

"His van was parked outside earlier." Tom nodded towards the craft block. "But I didn't see whether he was in his unit. I try to avert my eyes whenever I pass."

~

A short while later, David and I were back in the field, watching intently as Dougal strode across the expanse of grass and nettles. He held a metal divining rod in his hands and appeared to have his eyes closed.

"He's going to put his foot down a rabbit hole soon," David muttered.

"Can't he divine them? Or doesn't that thing work for holes?"

"I don't think it works for anything. In fact, I have no idea why we are even standing here," David complained. "You said earlier we were wasting our time. This has to be the biggest waste of time ever."

"Maybe," I agreed, "but he really wanted to help. It seems a bit rude to walk off and leave him to it."

But David had had enough.

"Then you stay and watch. I'll be in the Devon Mysteries when you get bored."

I stamped my feet as I watched him go and wondered how long I should wait before I, too, made my excuses and went back to the house.

Dougal was still walking, taking slow, measured paces, the divining rod pointing ahead of him like a tiny radar antenna. I had no idea how it was supposed to work, but I couldn't help but be impressed by Dougal's confidence in its power. He had not told us he would try to find the stopcock, or that he would do his best. He had simply agreed that he would find it for us.

Now as I watched him, I wondered what I should say when he failed. Should I thank him for trying and say perhaps it would have worked if he had longer to search? Or if the weather had been better? Or if the grass had been cut?

"It's here," Dougal called across. "Shall I put down a marker for you?"

I hurried across and stared down at the small metal plate. It was barely twenty centimetres across and had been buried beneath layers of mud and stones.

"That's incredible. However did you do it?"

"I didn't do anything," Dougal replied. "I just followed the rod. Were you looking for anything else?"

"No. That's all, thank you."

"In that case, I'll get back and have my lunch. If there's anything else I can do, just give me a shout."

He marched back to the craft block, and I was left with the strange feeling all the certainties in my life had crumbled to dust.

"But how did he do it?" I persisted. "Do you think he knew it was there all along? But how could have known? Was it some sort of act?"

"Does it matter?" Dad asked. "The flood has stopped and if there are any problems in the future, we know where to look for the stopcock."

"But that's not the point!" I wailed. "I want to understand!"

Dad grinned.

"Listen, love. If I've learned one thing about life, it's this. We'll never understand everything. Me, I gave up trying to make sense of the universe a long time ago. When something comes along that helps me, I just say, 'thank you, God,' and get on with it."

"You do believe in God, then?"

"I guess someone must have made everything. I don't think he lives in a church or a mosque, but sometimes, if I'm out in the woods or by the sea, I can believe there's something there with me."

"I wish I felt like that," I said plaintively. "I just don't believe any of it."

"Then don't believe. Just be glad the flood's stopped and we can get back to work."

"You're right. I should get on." I gave him a big hug, kissed his whiskery cheek, and headed back to the office.

Now the freeze was over and work had resumed, I should have felt better, but try as I might, I couldn't escape a sense of impending doom.

It didn't seem to matter how hard we worked. We kept slipping farther behind schedule.

It didn't help that Claire was teething and Bob and I were hardly getting any sleep. During her first year, Claire had been a very easy baby. She had been content, fed well, and slept through the nights. Now everything changed. Her cheeks flared with angry red patches and her gums swelled with one new tooth after another.

Nights had become an agony of endless hours walking around the bedroom, trying to soothe her to sleep only for another wave of screaming to start the moment she was laid in her cot.

I had never been so tired. I could still cope with physical tasks, but concentrating on paperwork was impossible. The moment I sat down, my eyelids drooped and the figures swam before my eyes.

Michael was teething too, and I knew David and Philippa were suffering similar problems. Late one afternoon, as I passed David in the downstairs corridor, I noticed he looked pale.

"What's the matter? Is something wrong?" I asked.

David shook his head. It was unlike him to be lost for words.

"Tell me what's going on," I urged him, but he said nothing until he had looked all around to make sure we could not be overheard.

"I wasn't going to tell anyone," he said, "but I just saw the weirdest thing."

"What?"

"It sounds ridiculous. I don't even know how to explain it, but I just saw someone wading through the floor."

"I don't understand."

"I can't explain it any better than that. I was going along the downstairs corridor and there was someone in front of me. I assumed it was one of the builders wearing a brown coat, but then I noticed there weren't any feet."

"How do you mean?"

"I told you, it's hard to explain. It wasn't exactly that it didn't have any feet. It was more as if the floor was made out of liquid and it was wading through it."

David really was looking ill.

"We're all too tired at the moment," I said. "Do you think you could have been imagining it?"

"Maybe..."

I put an arm around him.

"I think you need a break. It's lunchtime now anyway. Why don't you put your head down for an hour?"

He nodded.

"You're right. I have been feeling the pressure a bit. Look, don't mention this to anyone, will you? I don't want people thinking I'm cracking up."

"Of course not," I agreed. "I promise."

As he walked away, it dawned on me I had been so preoccupied by the freezing weather in recent weeks I hadn't thought about Fred at all. I hadn't even noticed hearing any footsteps around the house.

~

That night, as I undressed for bed, I noticed a folded piece of paper tucked under my pillow. Opening it, I saw a hand-drawn heart and the words "Sorry I didn't have a chance to get a proper card but you will always be my valentine xxx".

I sat on the edge of the bed and cried.

With everything that had been going on, it had completely escaped me that today was Valentine's Day.

Usually, Bob and I would do something to mark the occasion even if it was only a quiet meal at home, but this year I had completely forgotten.

At that moment, I felt a complete failure.

Everything I had worked so hard to achieve was hanging in the balance and it seemed my dreams were drifting out of reach. For months, I had barely stopped for breath. There had been no time to spend with Bob and no energy to play with Claire.

While I was pregnant, I had dreamed of relaxing with my

baby, reading books and playing with toys, but now I only fed her, changed her nappy and plonked her back in her playpen while I worked. It was not how I had wanted things to be.

And Bob saw even less of me than Claire did. Apart from our regular family meetings when we discussed how the building work was progressing, I rarely saw him from the moment I climbed out of bed in the morning to the moment I hit the pillow and slid instantly into an exhausted slumber at night. Whatever had happened to us?

I was still sobbing when Bob came in.

"What's the matter?"

"Nothing," I lied. "It's just that I don't have a card for you either."

He sat down beside me and lifted a strand of hair away from my face. "It doesn't matter. Cards aren't important right now. In a few weeks this rush will be over and everything will be easier."

"Do you really believe that?"

He put his arms around me, and my tears flowed uncontrollably.

"It's all such a mess," I sobbed. "We're never going to be ready to open on time, are we?"

"Of course we are. We have to be. We've put the date on all the posters."

"But it's not possible!" I howled. "Even if we work day and night, we will never get it done. It's hopeless."

He pulled a tissue from his pocket and wiped my tears.

"We can't give up now."

"I'm sorry…" I began, but he stopped me.

"No more words. Just get into bed and sleep."

Work continued and one morning Philippa asked me to help her mark out the lines for some extra fencing in the Animal Meadow. As we trudged up the hill with Ossie and Dino behind us, a man was walking down the track from the top field. He was tall, well over six feet, with broad shoulders and the confident swagger of someone who is used to being obeyed.

His broad face was deeply tanned and topped by a luxurious thatch of ginger-blonde hair.

"Good morning, girls," he boomed as we approached, "taking your dogs for a walk on my land, are you?"

I bristled at once.

"No," I replied coldly. "Actually, I was wondering what you are doing on our land."

"Your land? I don't think so," the man snorted. "I've just bought Norbrook Caravan Park, so I think you'll find this land belongs to me now."

"And I think, if you look at your plans, you will find that Norbrook land ends the other side of that fence."

"Yes," Phil joined in, "we bought Stokelake House months ago and these fields go with it."

"You bought Stokelake House, did you? Then you must be two very rich little girlies."

I was twenty-five years old and had just invested everything I had ever earned, as well as taking on a worrying amount of debt, to fund a share in my dream business. I did not appreciate being called a rich little girlie.

"What are you doing here?" I asked, trying to keep my voice controlled and business-like.

"I guess I'm making friends with my new neighbours," the man grinned. "I don't know if you've heard, but we have a very nice bar in the clubhouse. Maybe you two would fancy coming up for a drink sometime?"

I didn't wait to check with Phil. "No, thank you. We're far too busy preparing for our opening."

"Well, just ask at reception if you change your mind." He flashed a wide smile at us both. "The name's Matthews, by the way, Duncan Matthews."

He held out a hand, but I knew he was mocking me. Reluctantly, I shook his hand and his fingers clamped tightly over mine. I longed to pull away, but I didn't want to show how uncomfortable he was making me feel.

Finally, he released my hand and turned and ambled carelessly back up the track.

"What a horrible man," Phil said as we watched him go.

"Yes," I agreed. "Let's keep that gate locked from now on."

~

The first day of March dawned bright and crisp, and the sunlight brought a promise that spring was finally on the way.

Bob had looked after Claire during the night, and I had enjoyed the luxury of a few hours' sleep. I longed to bury my head under the pillow and stay in bed for the rest of the day, but when the alarm sounded, I struggled out and pulled on some clothes.

I knew there was a mountain of paperwork waiting to be done. In the past, Mum had always kept the books for the business, but then our accounts had been relatively simple. Now, with so many contractors working on the site, building regulations to follow, permissions to request, advertising to think about, VAT returns to submit and monthly budget updates to send to the bank, the workload had ballooned out of all proportion.

And while we were behind with our work schedule, we were ahead of ourselves with our spending. There had been all sorts of unexpected expenditures, and I was certain there would be more. We knew the only way to get back on schedule was to bring in extra workmen, but it meant increasing the amount we were spending, and I was reluctant to go back to the bank and ask for more money.

There had to be something we could cut back on. I was determined not to panic, but time was short. If we were going to get back on track, we needed to make changes now.

Mum and I were sifting through a mountain of invoices when Bob stuck his head around the office door.

Claire was in her playpen beside me and gurgled happily at the sight of him.

"I thought you might like some good news," he said. "The water problem has been solved."

"Seriously? How?"

"Your friend Dougal did it again. I noticed he was wandering around the field earlier with that stick of his and it seems he's found the spot where the water pipe's damaged. The plumber happened to be in today, working on the new loos, so I got him to take a look. We had to dig down a long way to find the pipe, but believe it or not, Dougal was right. It's a simple fracture, and the plumber reckons he'll have it all sorted by lunchtime."

I breathed a sigh of relief.

"That's fantastic! Maybe things are going to work out after all."

"Yes, that's wonderful news." Mum sounded as happy as me. "If everyone's got their water supply back, we won't have to worry about difficult neighbours anymore."

Bob grinned and blew a kiss to Claire as he closed the door.

I enjoyed a brief moment of contentment until a new thought burst into my head.

"Oh, God!" I gasped.

"What is it?" Mum asked.

"Have we had a water bill yet?"

"No, I don't think so. Why?"

"Do you know if our supply is on a water meter?"

"I've no idea."

"But if it is, and there are eight other properties, including a farm, going through the meter, does that mean we have to pay for all their water?"

"Surely not. They must be separated somehow. They must be…"

I hoped she was right, but my stomach churned.

"We'd better find out. Right now."

CHAPTER 12

My fears were soon confirmed.

In the undergrowth beside the road, a huge new mains water supply had been installed, complete with a meter, but the massive pipe was not connected to anything. Presumably it had been intended for the planned development at Stokelake House.

Beside it, a smaller, ancient-looking meter was attached to a pipe that ran first to Stokelake House and then to the other properties along the valley.

"This is crazy!" I wailed down the phone to our solicitor. "You can't seriously tell me we have to pay for all the water these other people use? Not to mention the water that's been escaping underground from the burst pipe? It's not right. Why didn't anyone tell us about it?"

"I really am very sorry." He had the grace to sound embarrassed. "We had no reason to suspect this situation existed."

"Surely that's the whole point of doing searches!" I snapped. "There has to be something we can do."

"I suppose you could put a separate meter on Stokelake House itself," he said at last. "If you did that, you could deduct the amount of water you were using from the total amount going through the meter and bill the other users for the remainder."

"Yes!" I pounced on the idea. "That's brilliant. Then we could pay our part and they could pay the rest to the water board themselves."

"Er... No. I'm afraid it wouldn't work like that."

"Why not?"

"Well, the responsibility still rests with you to pay the full amount to the service provider. In this case, the water authority. You would need to collect money from all the other users and make sure it was paid on time each quarter."

"What?!" I exploded again. "How are we supposed to do that? We don't even know who these people are! And how are we supposed to know how much water each of them has used? I'm sure they don't have individual meters. And even if they did, do you seriously expect us to go around and read them and work out how much they need to pay? Every few weeks? And what if they refuse?"

I stopped for breath, and the solicitor took his chance to apologise again.

"I really am sorry, Mrs Townsend, but this is a very unusual situation."

"No, it's not!" I was off again. "You told me it often happens with old estates that have been broken up. Surely you should have been aware there might be something like this and have checked it out? That's the whole point of having a solicitor, isn't it? To look into things? How much water is a farm likely to use, for God's sake? We can't afford this."

"If you want to make a complaint against my company..." he began, but I was too upset to listen.

"A complaint won't change anything, will it? Is there any point in explaining it all to the water board? Do you think they would let us just pay our part of the bill?"

His hesitation was all the answer I needed.

"No, of course they won't," I moaned.

"Mrs Townsend..." The solicitor was still trying to sound reassuring. "I think there is only one realistic answer to this situation. I know it's not ideal, but my suggestion is that you complete the new supply yourselves. If you lay a pipe from the new meter to Stokelake House and disconnect yourselves entirely from the existing supply, you will be able to approach the water authority and ask them to treat the two supplies separately."

"Would they do that?"

"They're not obliged to do it, but, in the circumstances, I think there is every chance that they would agree."

"But how much would it cost? It's a long way to run the pipe, and it's up the side of a hill. Who's going to pay for it?"

"I'm afraid that would be your responsibility."

"Then we can't win, can we? Either we pay a fortune for everyone else's water or we pay a fortune to put in a new water supply."

"I really am very—"

I slammed the phone down.

For a long time, I sat, head in hands, trying to control the panic inside me.

Finally, I went and found Mum.

She listened as I ranted about solicitors, searches and unreasonable neighbours, until I ran out of things to say.

"It's just so unfair," I ended lamely.

She gave me a hug, and I rested my head on her shoulder.

"Everyone's got enough to deal with already," I muttered. "They don't need any more bad news. We're supposed to be creating a happy family attraction. How can we do that if we're stressed out and exhausted all the time? Right now, I feel like painting the walls black and smashing the windows."

"Don't do that. It wouldn't help."

"It might make me feel better," I sniffed miserably.

"No, it wouldn't. Do you want me to upset you even more?"

I didn't answer.

"We can't stop," Mum said quietly. "That's the only thing that matters. We have to get this place open on time. If we don't, we're going to lose everything."

She pulled away and looked straight into my eyes.

"We can worry about the water supply later. We have six weeks left and everyone is exhausted. I need you to help me. It's up to us to raise everyone's spirits. We have to believe what we're doing is still possible and we have to make the others believe it, too."

~

Mum was serious about lifting people's spirits. She insisted the whole family met for lunch every day and for a cup of tea mid-morning and mid-afternoon.

The meetings had to be cheerful times when we could share progress. Problems could be discussed, but answers had to be found. No moaning was allowed.

Fortunately, tired as we were, we managed to keep a sense of humour, and Dad, in particular, managed to find something funny in every situation. Looking back, I can see those short times together really did keep us going.

~

It was during one of our family tea breaks that Bob made an announcement. He had been speaking to various coach companies about bringing groups to visit Silverlands and had just heard that one of the largest tour operators in the area had agreed to add us to their list.

We were all delighted, but I could see from Bob's expression he was hiding something.

"What's the catch?" I asked.

"It's not a catch, exactly, but there is a complication," he admitted. "They need a three-minute film of Silverlands to include in their advertising."

"How soon do they need it?"

"That's the problem. They want to send a camera team over this week..."

"No way!" David exploded. "That's impossible!"

"Don't panic. I've told them we can film something ourselves," Bob said.

"No, we can't!" David protested. "What are we supposed to film? Nothing's ready."

I tried to sound positive.

"There must be something..."

"Like what? It's all chaos!" David snapped.

"But if we don't send something by the end of the week, it'll be too late." Bob shot back.

"And it could make a big difference to us," I said quickly. "They bring thousands of tourists to Devon every year."

"So what? It's not possible!" David shouted.

Suddenly, my patience snapped.

"Stop being so negative!" I yelled at him. "We'll have to find a way, won't we?"

"Jesus Christ! You're impossible!" David shouted as he stormed out of the room.

~

When tempers had cooled, Mum put the kettle back on.

"It's a good thing we assembled the circus when we first moved in," she said cheerfully. "At least we can film that."

David only grunted.

"We could show Claire and Michael with the baby goats," Phil suggested. "They're really cute."

"Is anything finished in the First World War exhibition?" Dad asked.

"No," David said firmly. "The power hasn't been connected yet. The only lights are the neon tubes, so it would look awful."

"Could we use the Devon Mysteries?" Mum suggested.

"Possibly." Bob nodded. "The exhibits are all very dark, but we could try them with some extra lighting."

"Would that work?" I asked.

"There's only one way to find out. I'll get the camera and set up some lights."

The results were surprisingly good, and even David looked more hopeful.

"Sorry about earlier," I mumbled when we were alone.

"Yeah, me too," he replied.

News of the filming had spread to the craft block and everyone was eager to show off their products. Tom the Potter even managed a smile for the camera.

It was lunchtime when the phone rang. Bob answered it and came back with a worried expression.

"That was the coach company," he said. "They're happy for us to do the filming ourselves, but there's one thing they forgot to mention. Apparently, they like to include a shot of one of their coaches arriving at the location. I tried to talk them out of it, but they insisted."

"What does that mean?" I asked.

"Well, I told them we're filming today, so they're sending a coach over. It should be here in about an hour."

David nearly choked on his sandwich.

"I told you we'd never get away with it," he spluttered. "The outside of the house looks awful. The driver will take one look and leave."

"Not necessarily." Dad was as optimistic as ever. "Maybe we can get him to park the coach by the entrance, so it masks the rest of the building."

"I'll have a chat with him when he gets here and try to get him onside," Bob promised.

"And if the coach is going to be here in less than an hour, maybe it would be a good idea to move the builders' rubble and the concrete mixer and everything away from the front door?" Mum suggested.

We were still stacking scaffold boards and sweeping lumps of render from the tarmac when the coach drove in through the gates. As I looked up at the old house, my heart sank. Despite all the work we had done, it still looked derelict with drooping guttering and the gaping holes in the render that were still waiting to be repaired. I couldn't see how anyone would believe it could be ready to welcome guests in less than a month.

The driver pulled the coach to a halt, and I watched as Bob introduced himself. I didn't want to hear what was said, so I busied myself loading the last cement bags onto a wheelbarrow and trundled them around to the back of the building.

By the time I got back, Bob and the driver were chatting as if they had been friends for years.

"This is my wife," Bob said as I approached. "Diana, this is Arthur. He's going to be one of our regular drivers and I've just explained that every time he visits, he will be welcome to have a free meal or a cream tea."

"Of course," I agreed, "glad to meet you."

"Maybe you could find Arthur a mug of tea and a biscuit while I get everything set up?"

"Sure," I agreed. "No problem."

As I led Arthur through the downstairs corridor, he told me about himself and his family. I couldn't believe that he didn't comment once on the bare floorboards, missing doors and rusting iron radiators.

"I'm afraid there's still a lot of work to do," I said apologetically.

"Yes, your husband told me you're a bit behind, but he seems very confident it's all going to be ready on time."

"Yes, we all are," I lied.

By the time I got back, Bob had the camera set up and I could tell by the look on his face he wasn't happy.

"What's the matter?" I asked.

"This is hopeless." He sighed. "Whichever way I frame it, you can still see great lumps of wall missing."

"How long do we have the coach for?" David asked suddenly.

"Arthur has to leave by four o'clock, so that gives us just over an hour."

"Leave it to me," David said mysteriously. "Film anything else you can and meet me back here in thirty minutes."

I looked at Bob, but he only shrugged as David hurried off along the drive.

Twenty minutes later, were filming in the Enchanted Forest when the throbbing roar of an engine came from outside.

"What on earth's that?" Bob asked.

Looking out of the window, I was amazed to see a tractor rolling along the drive, with David hanging onto the side of the cab.

"What on earth is he playing at?" I demanded.

Hurrying outside, I saw the tractor had a huge laurel bush, the size of a tree, strapped to its bucket.

“Fancy a bit of gardening?” David shouted over the noise of the engine.

“What are you doing?” I shouted back.

“Camouflage! If we can’t repair it, we can hide it!”

He stuck his head through the tractor window, and as he spoke to the driver, I could see him pointing to the front of the house. At once, the tractor changed direction and the great wheels ground their way across the lawn.

“He’s completely lost it this time,” I gasped.

As the tractor stopped by the main entrance, David jumped down and signalled to the driver.

“This is Alan, by the way,” he called to me. “He owns the farm along the road.”

“Lovely,” I said blankly as Alan waved at me. “Nice to meet you.”

I watched in disbelief as the farmer swung the laurel bush around in the air, then lowered it to the ground in front of the damaged render.

“There!” David was pleased with himself. “That’s perfect!”

“But how’s it going to stay there? You don’t plan to have the tractor in the shot, do you?”

“Of course not. I’m going to strap the tree to the verandah.”

“You can’t! It’ll bring the whole thing down.”

“No, it won’t. Have a little faith in me. The uprights are solid. I’ve checked.”

Behind me, Bob was focusing the camera.

“How does it look?” I asked.

“Surprisingly good,” he answered. “Here, have a peek.”

I squinted through the eyepiece and was relieved to see the greenery looked natural. The gaping hole in the wall had disappeared, and without it, the main entrance looked old and interesting instead of old and decaying.

“You see, I do have some good ideas.” David grinned. “And I’ve asked Martin and Peggy from the craft block to come over and pretend they're visitors getting off the coach."

"Perfect," Bob said happily. "Let's crack on and get this done."

~

The next day, Bob sent the footage over to the coach company and we were all delighted to hear they were happy with it. The manager even agreed to come to the official opening.

Everyone was happy, but I couldn't stop worrying about how much there still was to do.

I knew Bob had sent out invitations to the press, the local television stations, other coach companies, tour operators, teachers, youth clubs, and members of the Chamber of Commerce. He was inviting everyone he could think of, and he expected me to share his excitement. I wanted to feel excited, I really did, but I just couldn't manage it. Every time I thought about the opening, my mind exploded with images of all the things that could go wrong.

~

I felt more hopeful when the builders started work on the tearooms.

The ground floor of the old carriage house had been converted into a kitchen for the school and it still had an impressive polished concrete floor, enormous steel sinks and a row of six ovens large enough to feed an army.

The glass was missing from one of the kitchen windows and pigeons had found their way inside and nested on top of the cupboards, but I knew it would soon be the perfect place to prepare delicious meals and snacks for our visitors.

All that was needed was to sweep away the piles of dead

leaves festering in the corners, steam-clean the black grease coating the ovens and the floor, unblock the sinks, sterilise the steel units, repaint the walls and ceiling and install new cupboards and work surfaces.

In addition, we needed to cut a doorway through into the adjoining room, which would become our servery.

We had chosen the room because it had a magnificent bay window and an elegant pair of French windows that opened onto the lawn. Once everything was finished, our tearoom would be able to seat forty people indoors and another sixty outside.

There was no point in trying to clean the kitchen until the hole in the wall had been knocked through. We knew the wall was substantial as it had originally been the exterior wall of the house, but we had no idea what materials it had been built from until we began work on it.

Paddy, a squarely built Irishman, was chosen to start the attack on the wall and, as he swung his sledgehammer, a shower of debris flew across the room. Within minutes, the ancient plaster lay scattered on the floorboards and the surface of the wall was revealed. I had expected to see bricks, but the wall appeared to have been built with anything that came to hand. There were rocks, large stones, a few bricks, and even some odd wooden blocks. At the bottom, there was a row of enormous rocks that could only be described as boulders.

"Jeez!" Paddy gasped as the dust cleared and he looked at the huge lumps of granite. "I wonder where they found those beauties."

Steve, the foreman, brushed away some of the remaining plaster.

"I'd guess they were already on site. It was probably easier to build them into the wall than move them out of the way. And it looks as if they had a spare gate post too."

He was right. A massive granite post was lying neatly

between the rocks and a rusted stump that had once been a hinge could be seen sticking out of one side of it.

"They didn't believe in wasting anything, did they?" Paddy chuckled.

"And you thought recycling was a new idea." Steve grinned back at him.

"That thing must weight tons," I said doubtfully. "Are you going to be able to move it?"

"It shouldn't be a problem." Steve was unconcerned. "If there's one thing Paddy's good at, it's knocking things down."

At that moment, the front doorbell echoed through the house. The bare floorboards and lack of furniture made the place reverberate like a drum and the dogs barked excitedly.

Opening the front door, I found Mr Turner from the planning department with two men I didn't recognise.

"Good morning," I said politely. "Can I help you?"

"I would like to introduce two of my associates from the Fire Department," Mr Turner said formally, "and while I'm here, I can check how the building work is going."

"Of course," I said, as my stomach tied itself into new knots. "Please, come in."

Trying not to let my voice betray my nerves, I asked Steve to join us and was relieved when he answered all of Mr Turner's questions about the way the building work was being carried out. I was starting to relax when the taller of the two fire officers asked me what our plans were regarding fire isolation. I shot a glance at Steve, but he only lifted his shoulders in the tiniest of shrugs.

"Can you give me some more details about that?" I asked, trying to hide my ignorance.

The taller of the two men explained that a whole raft of new regulations was about to come into force.

"Of course, you can ignore them for now, if you like," he said evenly. "They won't be implemented for another six months, but it would be a shame if you did all this work and then had to strip it all out again, wouldn't it?"

"So, what are these regulations, exactly?" Steve asked.

"It's all about safety," the second officer joined in. "It's about giving people time to leave the building. We need to know that if a fire breaks out, it will take at least an hour before it spreads anywhere else."

"Particularly between floors," the first man added.

"And how, exactly, do we do that?"

"There are lots of ways." The shorter man stepped forward as he warmed to his subject. "Each room must be isolated, which means the doors will need to be replaced by fire doors and they must be kept shut at all times. Furnishings and wall coverings must all be fire retardant and it's important that there are no sharp edges on the ceilings for the fire to get a grip on."

He pointed up at the intricate plaster designs above us. "Those mouldings, for instance. They will have to go. The easiest way would be to chisel them all off and paint the surface with fire-retardant paint, but you can line the ceiling with plaster board if you prefer."

I couldn't believe what I was hearing.

"And it's important to isolate any openings that could act as a chimney between floors," his companion added. "This staircase will need to be boxed in."

He waved an arm vaguely at the bottom step.

"It needn't be anything complicated. You could just fill in the railings, put a partition across here, and have a fire door at the top and bottom."

In my mind, I saw the elegant old staircase blocked away and hidden behind an ugly partition.

"No! We can't do that! This is an ancient building. It's beautiful. You can't just hack off the plasterwork and block in this magnificent staircase! It would be awful! Surely there are laws protecting places like this?"

"This place was under a demolition order until recently," Mr Turner reminded me. "I can assure you there is nothing protecting it."

"Then there should be!" I was outraged. "We are trying to restore this building and make it a beautiful attraction for people to visit. What you're suggesting would destroy the whole character of the house and turn the rooms into boring boxes. There must be something else we can do."

The three men exchanged glances.

"Our priority has to be safety," the tall man insisted. "If you don't want to do as we've suggested, the only alternative is to put fire proofing between the floors."

"Meaning?"

"It's a much more complicated process," Mr Turner explained. "You would literally have to lift every floorboard on the first floor, nail a metal grill between the rafters and fill the space with fire-retardant plaster."

I turned to Steve. "Is that possible?"

"I suppose so," he said doubtfully, "but that's an awful lot of floorboards."

"And you'd still have to block in the staircases," the short man added.

"But why?" I wasn't going to give in easily. "If we put a fire door at the end of the corridor upstairs, that would isolate the stairwell from the rest of the building. Why do we have to block in the bottom as well? All the downstairs rooms have doors leading straight outside, so they don't need another exit."

"That may be possible," the short man conceded, "but we will definitely need all the doors to be replaced by fire doors."

"Can we at least have them hooked back while we're open?" I begged.

"Only if they have automatic closers. That means

magnetic locks that close automatically if the fire alarms go off."

I dreaded to think how much a system like that would cost.

"Then that's what we will have. If it's the only way to preserve the building, we don't have any choice."

I held my head high as I showed the men out, then leaned against the wall. I knew Steve was watching me, but I couldn't hide how sick I felt.

"That's a bit of a blow, isn't it?" he said.

"You could say that," I agreed. "Just when I thought things couldn't get any worse."

"Oh, don't worry," Steve said, "things can always get worse."

His words did nothing to reassure me, so I took a deep breath and pulled myself up straight.

"Maybe we should check how Paddy's doing," I suggested.

~

We headed back to the soon-to-be tearoom, and, as I opened the door, I felt a low creaking sensation shiver through my legs. I didn't know what it meant, but Steve understood at once and jumped into action.

"You idiot!" he screamed at Paddy. "You were supposed to stack them outside, not on the bloody floor!"

A huge mound of boulders was piled in the middle of the tearooms floor and the ancient wooden boards creaked and groaned beneath their weight.

"Get the others!" Steve yelled at me. "Now! We've got to get these out of here before the floor gives way!"

He picked up an enormous rock and headed towards the French windows as I ran through the house, shouting for help.

By the time I got back with the others, Steve and Paddy were red-faced with exertion.

"Don't come close," Steve warned. "Stay there and we can pass them to you."

We made a human chain, handing the rocks from one to another across the room until they ended in a heap on the grass outside.

"I'm sorry, I should have thought," Paddy kept repeating. "They're not light, are they?"

None of us had enough breath to answer him.

Finally, when the mound had reduced to a pile of rubble and the floorboards had quietened, we stopped and stood panting, trying to get our breath back.

"I'm sorry about that," Steve turned apologetically to us, "I'd forgotten what a bloody idiot that man can be!"

CHAPTER 13

It was nearly lunchtime before I had a chance to tell the rest of the family about Mr Turner's visit.

"Well, that's it then." David's voice was loud with frustration. "We're finished. We might as well give up now."

"Calm down," Dad said. "Let's think for a minute. We've still got a few weeks."

"But we don't have enough time left to finish the work we're already doing already!" David complained. "We can't possibly take on anything else!"

"We could bring in more builders," Mum suggested.

"But how would we pay them? We're over budget now." I protested.

"Then we'll have to find things to cut."

The calmness of Dad's voice infuriated me.

"But we've already done that! You know we have! Because of the fiasco with the water supply, we've already cut everything."

"Then David's right and we give up." Dad looked at me. "Is that what you want? To give up now when we're so close?"

I couldn't speak. I knew he expected me to be strong, but

inside I was crumbling. The enormity of what we were up against felt overwhelming.

Bob must have sensed how I felt because he slipped his arm around my waist.

"We haven't confirmed the order for the kitchen equipment yet," he said. "Maybe we could have another look at that?"

"And the second stable block isn't due until next week," Philippa added. "We might still be able to cancel it. We'll have to delay the donkeys until next year."

"Okay." I blew my nose and tried to sound calm. "I guess we'd better get on with it, then."

It took nearly a week, and several more meetings with the fire officers, before we had a realistic cost for the extra work. It was devastating.

"I told you," David muttered, "we're finished."

"I know it looks bad," I agreed, "but I don't think we have any choice."

"If we pay for the extra building work, how much does it leave for everything else?" Bob asked.

"Nothing," I replied as I showed him the new projections. "Actually, it's less than nothing. I've cut everything that isn't absolutely essential, but we're still way over budget."

"Is there anything else we can do ourselves?" Mum asked.

"We could do a lot of the inside decorating," Bob suggested. "Apart from repairing the damage to the walls, it's mainly just painting and putting up wallpaper."

"I could do the carpentry work," David admitted, "but there's no way we could get it all done in time."

"Yes, there is," Dad replied. "We just have to give up sleeping."

For once, none of us saw the joke.

"Tom the Potter might help," I suggested, "especially if we offer to reduce his rent."

"That's a brilliant idea!" Bob burst out unexpectedly. "I've found plenty of craftspeople who want to move into the other units, but they're all struggling for money. I'm sure that if we offered them some rent-free time in return for working with us, they'd jump at the chance."

"And they're all creative," Phil joined in. "I bet they'd be really good at decorating."

Within days, we had a new team at work.

Our craftspeople were an eclectic bunch. They included a knitwear designer, two picture-framers, a wooden toy maker, a candlemaker and a family of glass engravers.

Their ages ranged from early twenties to late sixties, but they were united by a passion for life and a love of everything creative. And most important of all, they brought with them a wave of energy and optimism that lifted our spirits and brought us renewed hope.

The old building echoed with laughter once again and our lives developed a new routine. During the days we worked with the builders and craftspeople, pushing on with renovating and decorating, but then, once the others had left, the family snatched a hurried meal, settled the children down to sleep, and returned to work on the displays.

A new figure takes shape

David was busy making models that would bring the Down in Devon and First World War exhibitions to life, and Dad was creating the background scenes and panoramas.

Mum and I still had huge murals to paint on the walls of the Enchanted Forest, and Phil was setting up the interior of our new gift shop while Bob concentrated on advertising and promotions.

Each night we worked until we couldn't keep our eyes open any longer, then crept to bed, knowing our alarms would ring in a few short hours.

I can't speak for the others, but I know that when I did sleep, my dreams were so full of chaos and confusion I felt more tired when I woke up than when my head hit the pillow.

When we first saw Stokelake House, it had four staircases. In addition to the main flight in the entrance hall, there was another, less ornate staircase in the dormitory block at the back of the house. We weren't going to open that part of the site in the first year, so we didn't have to worry about it for the time being.

At the far end of the main building, a third staircase linked the Enchanted Forest with the Down in Devon display, and the fire officers agreed we could isolate it by adding fire doors at the top and bottom.

However, we ran into problems with the fourth staircase, which was a strange, twisted creation squeezed into the middle of the house. It was much narrower than the other stairways and had presumably been intended to be used by servants.

The fire officers were not impressed with it. They told me the steps were too deep, too narrow and too twisting. If we wanted to use it, we would have to enlarge the cavity, which would mean cutting into the adjoining rooms.

Any more expense was out of the question, so our only option was to board the staircase in.

I felt sad as I watched the builders hammering together a wooden frame and nailing sheets of plasterboard across the yawning entrance.

Once the staircase had been blocked in, and the plasterboard covered with wallpaper, no one could tell the old, worn steps were still gathering dust in the darkness, but every time I walked along the corridor, I found my eyes drawn to the new section of wall.

It made me feel strangely uncomfortable, as if the old house was keeping a secret.

~

A few days after the staircase was boxed in, David was replacing a damaged section of skirting board when he made a discovery. He dragged me along the corridor to show me what he had found.

"Look at this."

"Look at what?" I asked, seeing only the floorboards and a gap where the skirting board had been removed.

"Look at the levels," David urged. "There, through the gap. This isn't the original floor. It must have been put in later. If you look down, you can see the original was a lot lower."

There was a strange quality to his voice, and suddenly I understood what he was saying. "You mean the figure you saw?"

He nodded, and a shiver ran up my spine.

"It wasn't wading through the floor. It was walking on the old floor. That's why I couldn't see its feet."

"Have you seen it again?" I asked.

David shook his head, but I sensed he was hiding something.

"What is it?" I asked.

"I haven't seen anything, but I've started hearing footsteps again. Things seemed to have gone quiet, but yesterday it almost felt as if they were following me."

"It's probably just that we've got more people working in the house. You know how much everything echoes."

"I suppose so, but it is weird, isn't it? The floor I mean."

"Yes, but we really don't have time for this now."

David nodded.

"I know. I just wanted to show you. I won't tell anyone else."

~

That night, as I passed Dad in the corridor, I stopped for a few words.

"Everything okay?"

"Fine," he grumbled. "I just wish I could persuade your brother to switch off the lights. We're supposed to be saving money, but he keeps switching every light in the block on."

"Really?" I frowned disapprovingly. "I'll have a word with him."

David was installing the figures in the First World War exhibition, so I popped in as I passed.

Dad was right. The exhibition contained four separate rooms, and although David was only working in one of them, all four were ablaze.

"Me?" David looked outraged when I asked him about the lights. "I keep turning them off. If you need to talk to anyone about leaving the lights on, it's Dad."

I didn't want to provoke another argument, so I let the subject drop.

A few nights later, I was about to give up and go to bed

when I heard raised voices coming from the First World War exhibition.

As I hurried in, the first room was ablaze with light. So was the second. I followed the voices and found Dad and David in the third room.

"What's the matter?" I asked.

They looked at me, and I could see the tiredness in their faces.

"Nothing," Dad grumbled. "I've been trying to explain we need to stop using so much electricity."

"And I've been pointing out that it's not me!" David scowled.

"Look, we're all tired. Perhaps it's time to call it a night." I suggested.

They grunted irritably and followed me back towards the corridor. As we walked through the second room, there was a faint click of a switch and we were plunged into darkness.

"Bob? Is that you?" I called.

Silence.

"Mum? Phil? Can you put the lights back on, please?"

There was no answer, and for long moments, we stood wrapped in velvety blackness. I could hear the others breathing and a scuffle of footsteps told me David was feeling his way around the room. Finally, there was a click, and the lights flickered back on.

"Who did that?" David demanded.

"The switches in here must be ancient," Dad said. "Maybe one's worn. It would only take a vibration from somewhere to make it flip."

"And the emergency lights?" David asked. "They were off too."

Dads shook his head and turned away.

"Perhaps the electrician turned them off earlier. Either way, it's time to call it a night."

He gave me a hug before heading off to his flat.

"Are the switches really worn?" I asked David when Dad had gone.

"No. We've replaced all the wiring in here. The switches are brand new and the emergency lights were on when I came in."

"Then I don't understand.... What caused it?"

"I've no idea." David sighed. "But like I said, it wasn't me."

~

We had originally planned to build an impressive entrance kiosk by the main gate where people could buy their tickets before coming in. Unfortunately, it had been one of the first things to go in our cost-cutting exercise.

David managed to acquire a small, prefabricated garden shed from somewhere and assured us it would be easy to convert the window into a hatch and add a shelf with enough room for a till.

Mum had always been in the ticket box when the exhibition had been in the Spanish Barn and she had volunteered to keep the job once Silverlands was open.

"As long as I've got a roof over my head, I'll be fine," she insisted.

When the shed arrived, however, I looked at the pile of panels on the ground and my heart sank. It was certainly not going to be the entrance kiosk we had envisioned, but for the time being, it would have to do.

Steve and I were marking out the concrete base for the shed when an engine roared behind me.

As I swung around, a range rover swept past. The driver's window was open, and I caught a glimpse of Duncan Matthews. His voice floated back to me as the car headed along the drive to the house.

"Morning, Sweetie."

My irritation was tinged with curiosity and I left Steve mixing the concrete and headed back to the house.

As I approached, Bob was standing by the entrance and I saw Matthews pat him on the shoulder before climbing back into his Range Rover. He waved as he drove past.

"What was that all about?" I demanded, as I reached Bob.

"David and I have been invited up to the caravan park for a drink."

"Why?"

"No idea. But it can't do any harm, can it?"

The next afternoon, Bob and David headed up to Norbrook Caravan Park, and I found myself feeling unusually bad-tempered. I suspected there was a reason for the invitation and I couldn't concentrate until they came back.

When they returned, they looked worried.

"What did he want?" I asked, but Bob insisted we get everyone together.

"He was friendly enough to start with," David said as soon as the family was gathered. "He showed us around the place and told us how much money they've spent on everything."

"The facilities are pretty impressive," Bob admitted. "The swimming pool and leisure centre are amazing."

"But what did he want?" I repeated.

"He said he wanted to help us with our advertising."

"Some help." David cut in. "He started spouting figures, telling us how many visitors they get every year, how many days they stay, how much they spend in the restaurant, that sort of thing."

"Basically, he said that if a fraction of the people that visit them come down to visit Silverlands, it could make a huge difference to us."

"And?"

"He offered to put an advert on the back of the information leaflet they hand out to all their visitors."

"That sounds good," Phil said. "Would we have to pay for it?"

"That's the bad news."

"How much did he want?" Dad asked.

"Here." Bob put a piece of paper on the table. "See for yourselves."

I looked at the figures and gasped. "But that's more than half our advertising budget!"

"I know. I said we'd already committed our budget for this year, but he wouldn't let it go."

"What do you mean?"

"He kept asking what we were doing that was going to be as effective as his leaflets. I tried to change the subject, but in the end, I thought it best to be direct. I told him I've booked radio adverts, newspaper adverts and bus adverts. There will be posters in every hotel and guesthouse in South Devon and leaflets in all the tourist information centres."

"What did he say to that?"

"To be honest, it got a bit uncomfortable. He said what a shame it would be if none of his visitors came down to visit us."

"It was more than that," David complained. "He got quite threatening. He said we ought to remember that most of our business would be from their visitors. He said we'd be wasting money advertising anywhere else because no one would travel anywhere just to see a model exhibition."

Bob nodded.

"He said if word got around their site it wasn't worth coming down here, we probably wouldn't last the first season."

"What a bastard!" I gasped. "You mean he's trying to force us into paying for his crappy leaflets just to stop him bad-mouthing us?"

"Yes, that pretty much sums it up."

"What did you say?"

"Nothing. We walked out."

"He's just another bully," Dad sighed. "I've seen plenty of them in my time, but luckily, he doesn't have any power over us."

It was Bob who brought the subject up. I think he knew I had been avoiding it.

"We ought to advertise for staff soon. Do you want me to interview them, or are you going to do it?"

I didn't answer. To be honest, I would rather have run the tearooms on my own, but I knew it wasn't possible. The thought of sharing the kitchen and counter with people I didn't know made me very uncomfortable. I knew it was ridiculous, but it did.

"I don't mind doing the interviews," Bob went on, "but it would be better if it was you. After all, you're the one that's going to have to work with them."

"You don't have to remind me. Yes, I'll do it. It's not a big deal." I lied.

I think he knew how worried I was because he reached out and took my hand.

"Or we can do it together, if you'd rather."

"That would make sense. After all, they will have to work with you, too."

"In that case, I'll arrange some interviews. Is Friday all right for you?"

"Could we make it next Monday?"

"If you like," he agreed, "but why the delay?"

"I'll need the weekend to clean the kitchen. You know what a state it's in."

Bob frowned.

"But if we're taking on people to work in the kitchen, surely their first job will be to clean everything?"

"No. I have to clean it before they arrive."

"But that doesn't make any sense."

I wanted to explain, but I knew he wouldn't understand.

"I'm sorry, but it has to be that way. If people come into the kitchen when it's filthy and clean it all up, then it will feel like it's their kitchen, not mine."

"Oh, for God's sake!"

"I'm sorry. I'm not trying to be difficult. Please, just let me do it."

Bob shook his head in disbelief.

"You really are impossible sometimes."

I spent the entire weekend scraping and scrubbing the kitchen, but by Monday morning, everything was gleaming.

"That does look impressive," Bob admitted grudgingly. "Now you've worn yourself out, are you going to be able to stay awake for the interviews?"

"I'm fine," I said grumpily. "Let's get on with it."

~

Sheila, the first applicant, was in her thirties with a serious expression, knee-length skirt and flat lace-up shoes. I smiled at her hopefully, but after shaking my hand and introducing herself, she addressed all her questions to Bob.

She had worked in hotels, restaurants and care homes and wanted to know exactly how many staff would be working in the kitchen.

"We are thinking of three people altogether, but we may bring in some part-timers during the peak season," Bob replied, "depending on how things go."

Sheila did not look impressed.

"She seemed very organised," Bob said once she had gone.

"Yes, she did. Are there many more?" I asked.

"Lots."

Bob showed me a list of names and grinned at my expression. "Don't look so miserable. I'm sure they're all lovely."

Mandy, the next girl, was much younger, maybe seventeen, and never stopped talking. I thought she was nervous and tried to sound friendly, but I soon realised she was not listening to anything I said.

"Have you worked in a kitchen before?" I asked.

"My sister said I ought to apply. She works in the market in Newton Abbot and she's thinking of getting a new job herself. She's been there for ages and she says it's dead boring."

"Oh... and do you enjoy cooking?"

Mandy flicked her long blonde hair away from her face.

"My sister's called Tia. She's a bit of a headcase, really, but in a good way."

"I see. But she thinks this job would suit you?"

"Our Mum says we ought to work together in a nail bar because we're both artistic. I expect you can see that from my makeup."

I glanced across at Bob and saw he was shaking with suppressed laughter.

"And do you have any questions for us, Mandy?" I asked.

"No, not really."

I thanked her for coming and ushered her out of the door.

"This is hopeless," I sighed. "Do we really have to have staff?"

"Of course we do. There are eleven more on the list and if we don't find any that are right, I will put out another advert."

I knew Bob was trying to be encouraging, but I longed to throw open the French windows and run.

The rest of the morning was a procession of young women who answered our questions in polite voices.

Only one stood out, an earnest sixteen-year-old with a beaming smile who told us she loved cleaning things.

"You might have to tell me what to do a few times before I get it," she said. "My Mum says it's because I'm thick as porridge but I do work hard. Everyone says I work hard."

As she stood up to leave, she caught the leg of the table with her foot and scattered Bob's papers all over the floor. Her name was Abbie.

The last name on the list was Martha O'Rourke. By then, I was sinking into a pit of depression.

When the door opened and Martha walked into the room, the first thing that struck me was how tiny she was, not much over four feet tall, but the second thing I noticed was her vitality.

I guessed she was in her late fifties, or possibly even older, but there was an energy in her movements that had been missing from many of the younger women.

Her arms were thin but wiry and her face was worn but kind. I liked her at once. There was a Scottish lilt to her voice that sounded calm and confident.

I could tell she had impressed Bob as well because the moment she left, he turned and looked at me.

"What do you think?" he asked. "Do we need to go through them all, or are there any clear winners?"

"I think we both know, don't we?" I said. "It has to be Martha."

"I'm so glad you said that. I think she will be perfect. I'm not so sure about the second one, though. Were there any others that impressed you?"

"Definitely," I said without hesitating. "I know who I want for the kitchen."

"Do you? Which one?"

"Abbie. She's lovely."

"Really?" Bob looked horrified.

"She said herself that she's not very bright. Surely we could do better?"

"No. She'll learn. She says she's a hard worker and I believe her. I think she and Martha will make a great team."

"Are you sure?"

"Absolutely positive."

"Well, if you're certain." Bob hesitated. "Maybe it will be best to give her a trial period and see how it goes."

"If you like," I agreed, "but don't worry, she's going to be great."

Martha and Abbie started straight away. As Silverlands was going to be open seven days a week during the summer, we took on a couple of other girls to fill in the gaps and I felt more optimistic. Not only did we have a tearoom, but we had a team to run it. Surely nothing could go wrong now?

~

We had been so busy that it came as a surprise when I opened my bedroom curtains one morning and saw the grass bank outside was a mass of golden daffodils.

Spring had crept up on me, and I hadn't even noticed.

I felt a familiar shudder as I remembered how few days were left until our official opening, but I pushed away my fears and let myself focus for a moment on the beauty outside.

After breakfast, I took Claire to look at the wonderful sight. The grass bank stretched from the front of the house all the way along the main drive to the entrance gate and the changing seasons had transformed it into a magnificent array of wildflowers. In addition to the gently bobbing daffodils, there was a sea of blue wood anemones mixed with deep purple orchids and tiny dog-violets.

Here and there, I spotted another flower that I didn't recognise. Large, bell-like blooms hung from slender, drooping stalks, their petals dappled with intricate patterns of reds, pinks and purples.

I asked Claire if she knew their name, but she looked at me with huge brown eyes and giggled.

Back inside, I described the flowers to the others, but no one knew what they were.

Later that afternoon, Martha and I were unpacking a delivery of china when I glanced out of the window and noticed a group of men walking around the far side of the lawn.

Recognising the broad shoulders and straw-like hair of their leader, I wiped my hands on a towel, pulled on a coat, and headed out of the kitchen door.

Duncan Matthews saw me as I approached. He was holding a map and giving orders to four workmen who were hacking down the shrubbery at the side of the lawn.

"Oh look, it's the Ice Queen," he smirked.

"What the hell are you doing?" I demanded.

"If you must know, I've brought my team down to inspect the septic tank," he said, pointing to a row of metal plates sunk into the ground. "We don't need any help from you."

"But why are you cutting down our bushes?"

The workmen were watching the confrontation with interest. Matthews noticed and signalled them to get back to work.

"Did I tell you to stop?" he barked.

"And why are you on our land, anyway?" I persisted.

"Because I have a legal right to access my septic tank at any time I choose. If you have a problem understanding that, you'd better get your solicitor to explain it to you."

"I don't have a problem understanding," I retorted, "but it

seems you have a problem reading maps. This is our septic tank. Yours is on the other side of the drive."

There was a ripple of suppressed laughter from the workmen, and Matthew's expression darkened. Pulling open the map, he studied it for a moment, then pulled himself up to his full height.

"It wouldn't hurt you to be a little more neighbourly, Missy," he snarled.

"And it wouldn't hurt you to be a little less rude."

~

A few days later, I took Claire over to the Animal Meadow to meet the new arrivals. In addition to the baby goats, we had been loaned two orphan lambs by a local farmer. They were named Dot and Daisy and were absolutely adorable. They bleated constantly and were full of mischief, upturning buckets of feed and playing with anything they could find.

Rabbits and guinea pigs arrived soon afterwards, together with chickens, bantams and geese.

Two miniature Vietnamese pot-bellied pigs arrived next. They were both black and hairy and as round as they were bristly. They were very friendly and well-behaved except for their habit of knocking Phil off her feet in their rush for food.

I hadn't expected the animals to make so much noise. They weren't so loud they were distracting, but whenever I was outside, there was a distant clucking or mewing. I loved it. It made the whole place feel alive, and I knew the new additions were going to be very popular with the public.

The only members of the family that didn't like the animals were the dogs.

On the day the pigs arrived, Dino and Ossie barked with excitement as the lorry drove past the front of the house.

They must have picked up the unusual smell, as they normally ignored delivery vans.

Later, when I opened the door of the Enchanted Forest, Dino pushed past me and went haring across to the Animal Meadow. He stopped with his nose pressed against the wire of the pig enclosure and quivered with excitement.

"Come back here!" I shouted as I chased after him, but Dino was immovable. His eyes were huge and his nose was pushed halfway through the wire mesh, his nostrils flaring at the scent of the amazing creatures.

Phil was busy with the morning feed.

"I don't know what's going on up there," she said, pointing up the hill towards Norbrook, "but there's been a team working all morning. They've brought in JCBs, so they must be doing something major."

Beyond our fence, the land dipped and I could see men's heads moving and the arm of a JCB swinging from side to side.

"I think they're building something," Phil said, but I wasn't convinced.

"Surely we would have heard? They would have to get planning permission for any sort of a building, and I'm sure Mr Turner would have mentioned it."

To my surprise, Mr Turner had become a regular visitor and had even become something of a friend. He had offered advice on several difficult subjects, and each time, his suggestions had saved us time and money.

"Well, perhaps you should ask him if he knows what's going on next time you see him," Phil said.

Despite the odd noises and the builders' ghostly stories, I never felt uncomfortable walking through the corridors of Silverlands late at night. I wasn't worried me about coming face to face with a ghost, but early one morning, I turned a corner and was confronted by something that was very much alive.

For a moment, I thought it was a cat, with a thick coat of dark fur, intelligent eyes and long whiskers. It seemed as surprised to see me as I was to see it, because it made no attempt to run away but stood its ground and considered me with its head tilted to one side.

It was only when it lost interest and turned to walk away that I saw a long, tapering pink tail swing around behind it.

There was no doubt. It was a rat. And it was enormous.

I had no idea rats could grow to such a size, and for a moment, I stood transfixed. Coming to my senses, I hurried after the creature, but found it had already disappeared into the shadows. For a moment, I wondered if I had been dreaming, but I knew I had not. Its bright eyes and inquisitive expression were still fresh in my memory.

There was nothing I could do for the time being, so I decided to go to bed and tell the others in the morning.

But I didn't have to tell the others about the rat. By the time I came downstairs, everyone was gathered in the kitchen and Phil was in tears, explaining that the Animal Meadow was overrun. There were rats in the stable, rats in the food store and rats in the aviaries and animal runs.

"Where have come from?" David demanded. "It's like a plague!"

Bob was already on the phone to the pest control people.

"They'll be here as soon as they can," he said as he finished.

"But what are we going to do?" Mum asked. "They're everywhere! I chased one out of the office earlier and Dad found some in the gents' loos."

"Look, there's one down there by the footpath," Phil said, peering out of the window.

Dad joined her and watched another rat scamper across the lawn.

"We can't get distracted. There's no time. We have to keep working."

"But we can't just ignore them!" David protested.

"Yes, we can," Dad said firmly. "That's exactly what we're going to do."

~

"You won't believe this!" David fumed as he burst through the office door. "I know where the rats have come from. It was Matthews! The previous owners up at Norbrook were dumping all their waste rather than paying to have it removed. They'd made an illegal landfill site just up the hill from us and now he's clearing it. That's what the JCBs are doing."

I did believe it. It was exactly the sort of thing I could imagine him doing.

"And all their rats have moved down here? Surely we can sue him?"

"I doubt it," David said miserably. "All he's done is clear an illegal dump. It was the last owners that were in the wrong, not him."

"He must have known what would happen. And he knows we're about to open. It's not a coincidence, is it?"

"No, of course, it isn't."

"What a bastard!" Pushing back my chair, I jumped to my feet. "I'm going up there right now and I'm going to tell him…"

But David caught my arm.

"No, you're not. Dad was right. There's no time. There's still loads to do. Forget the rats. Forget Matthews. We just have to keep going."

It was late in the afternoon before the pest controllers arrived. I had expected an army of exterminators and my disappointment must have shown when I opened the front door and found a small man in a white coat and his teenage assistant.

"Don't worry, Madam, we know what we are doing," the man said when I asked if they would be able to cope with the whole property.

I had never been called "Madam" before and I felt a little offended.

"But there are over sixty rooms, and there are hundreds of rats."

"Yes," the man's eyes widened as he saw a shape dart along the corridor behind me, "and they're impressively large, aren't they?"

I explained about the illegal dump and the man nodded.

"That would explain it," he said. "I expect they've been living up there for years with a steady supply of food, undisturbed, able to breed in peace. It's no wonder they're so big. They've been living in a little rat Utopia."

"But now they're here. Can you get rid of them?"

"We certainly can, Madam. The first thing we need to do is to decide on our strategy. Do you prefer to go with traps or poison?"

"What's the difference?" I asked.

"Both are effective but, with a property this big, it may take weeks or even months to trap them."

"Months? We're opening to the public this weekend!" I wailed. "We can't open a tourist attraction that's infested with rats!"

"Then it's going to have to be poison," the man said firmly. "That will do the trick. We'll get started right away."

An image of my night visitor flashed into my mind, and

as I remembered the way his intelligent little eyes had considered me, I felt awful that I was agreeing to exterminate him and his relatives.

The rest of the family felt differently. They had no sympathy for the rodents at all.

Even the dogs seemed wary of the invaders. I had expected them to chase the rats the moment they saw them, but they made no attempt. They could clearly smell the rats, as their noses were constantly twitching with excitement, but whenever they spotted one, they simply barked loudly and stayed exactly where they were. Perhaps they knew how sharp a rat's teeth can be.

After forty-eight hours, the number of rat sightings dropped dramatically. There was still the occasional flash of a tail or a shadow running along a corridor, but even though we didn't see them, we could still hear them.

There were constant swishings, patterings and gnawings from behind the walls and under the floorboards. If you stood quietly and listened, it seemed the house itself was alive with rustling. When the new heating system was installed, the plumbers had left the Victorian pipes in the walls and the rats used them to move from one part of the house to another.

"It's horrible," I said to Dad as we worked in the Down in Devon exhibition. "I feel so guilty about poisoning them. It's not their fault they're rats."

"Then try not to think about it. I know you love animals, but I'm afraid humans and rats don't mix."

I sighed.

"I know, but I still hate it."

CHAPTER 14

Silverlands was due to open to the public on Easter Sunday, but we had planned a special preview for the press and invited guests on Saturday. Lots of our guests had already RSVP'd saying they were coming, so it was essential we made a good impression. The success or failure of Silverlands depended on it.

On Tuesday morning, the carpet layers arrived.

There were six members in the team and they all wore immaculate grey overalls with red belts and matching baseball caps.

Their leader was a thin, unsmiling man called Timothy, who asked me endless questions and wrote all my answers on his clipboard.

He seemed very neat and organised, and I wondered how he felt about rats.

Weeks ago, when he had visited to give us a quote for the work, Timothy had said it would take three days for the carpet layers to work from one end of the building to the other and he had been very clear that every room must be completely empty before they began work.

I had assured him that would not be a problem, but now, as the team unloaded their gear from the van, I knew Steve and Paddy were still upstairs finishing the fireproofing. They were in the last room of the Down in Devon section and had promised they would be finished by lunchtime. I suggested the carpet layers began at the other end of the house and kept my fingers crossed.

It wasn't long before I heard raised voices and hurried upstairs.

Paddy was kneeling by an open section of floor pouring plaster between the joists while Timothy glared down at him.

"...and I'd get it done a whole lot faster if I wasn't wasting my time arguing with you," Paddy muttered darkly.

"Is there a problem?" I asked.

"There certainly is," Timothy rounded on me. "I need to get my men in here to start prepping the floor. You told me this room would be empty."

"It will be empty soon," I assured him. "That's why I suggested you start at the other end of the building."

"We don't just unroll the carpet and stick it down, you know." Timothy protested. "There's a lot to prepare. We have to level the surface, prime it, fix the underlay. It all takes time."

"Does it now? Fancy that..." Paddy muttered.

"The upstairs corridor is clear," I said quickly. "You can do that next, if you like. I'm sure this room will be ready by the time you're finished."

"Sorry about that," I said to Paddy once the carpet layer had gone. "Keep going, you're doing a great job."

Paddy smiled wryly up at me.

"Never you mind about him. He can't help it that God made him an arsehole. Have you seen any rats today?"

"I haven't," I replied, "but David spotted one downstairs earlier."

"They must have been in here last night. Look at this, the little buggers."

He held out a hammer and I could see the end of the wooden handle had been chewed to shreds.

"Oh dear, I'm sorry."

"I know. It's bad enough with Fred playing tricks on me without the rats joining in."

Usually I avoided talking about the ghost, but my curiosity got the better of me.

"What's happened now?"

"I left a pile of nails in here last night, all ready to finish these boards, but they've gone. Vanished."

"Could the rats have taken them?"

"Why would they? They can't eat nails. No, I'm thinking it was Fred just winding me up."

"Well, whatever it was, make sure you're finished in here before the carpet layers come back."

"To be sure, I will," Paddy grinned. "I don't want to be getting into any arguments, now, do I?"

Leaving Paddy to finish the fireproofing, I headed to the Devon Mysteries exhibition where Dad was installing a display about the Hairy Hands of Dartmeet, the phantom hands that are said to grab the steering wheel of unsuspecting drivers and crash their vehicles into the river Dart.

We had decided not to carpet the floor in this exhibition, as the echo of footsteps added an extra dimension of creepiness to the rooms.

Dad was lying on the floor, working on a mechanism that would make the ghostly hands appear whenever anyone approached.

"How are things?" he asked when he saw me.

"Not great," I replied. "Paddy's itching to pick a fight with the carpet layer and there are still rats everywhere."

"Forget the rats," Dad said. "Let the experts deal with them."

"I can't forget them! I'm worried about the carpet layers. If they realise the place is infested, they'll probably walk out."

"No, they won't. This is a big job for them. They've got a vanload of carpet outside, so even if they make a fuss, they'll get the job done."

"I hope you're right. I have a horrible knot in my stomach as if I'm waiting for disaster to strike."

Dad chuckled. "You worry too much. Remember, we're nearly there now."

"I know, but I can't believe it's possible to feel this tired and still be conscious."

"Maybe you're not conscious. Maybe this is all just a bad dream and you're going to wake up any minute and find yourself back in the Barn."

"Don't say that," I pleaded. "I'm struggling to keep in touch with reality as it is."

"What's that old saying? You don't have to be mad to work here, but if you are, it helps."

"That ought to be our motto," I agreed. "Perhaps we should have it painted above the front door."

Later that morning, when I went back to check on the carpet layers, I was amazed to see the difference the new floor covering made to everything.

Instead of walking over dirty, scarred floorboards, I found myself stepping onto an expanse of clean, honey-coloured carpet.

It looked wonderful and brought out the best in everything. For the first time, I noticed how bright and welcoming the rooms looked now they had been redecorated, and how the paint on the doors and skirting boards glistened under the sparkling new light fittings.

A surge of pride lifted my spirits. Despite all the obstacles, we had accomplished so much. If only we could keep up the pace for a few more days, we would be ready to welcome our first visitors.

By the end of the afternoon, the carpet layers had completed all the upstairs rooms and were ready to start the main staircase when they returned in the morning.

I watched them go before heading back to the kitchen to prepare a meal for Claire. I really hoped she would sleep through the night as I still had half of the murals in the Enchanted Forest to paint.

Claire was usually a good eater, but, as I put her food in front of her, she grabbed the bowl and tipped it onto the floor.

"What was that for?" I asked indignantly, then my heart sank as I saw the familiar red patch on her cheek and a trickle of dribble escaping from the corner of her mouth.

"Oh no," I groaned, "don't tell me you've got another tooth on the way?"

Bob and I took it in turns to sit with Claire while she tossed and cried through the night. I got a few hours of sleep, but by the morning, I wanted to bury my head under a pillow and cry. Every fibre of my being was at breaking point. There were three days left until we opened and we still had a mountain to climb to have everything ready.

"Good morning!" Abbie trilled as I walked into the kitchen. "I thought it might help if I came in a bit early. Do you want me to get you some breakfast?"

My tiredness made me emotional, and tears welled at this unexpected kindness.

"No, I'm not hungry, thanks, but I'd love a cup of tea."

"Okay," she replied, "but you really ought to eat something. You have to keep your strength up."

I knew she was right, but the thought of food made me feel sick. I hadn't eaten a full meal in days.

"OK. I'll make myself some toast."

"I'll do it." Abbie beamed. "And I'll do some scrambled eggs and beans to go with it. You look after the baby."

I was settling Claire into her playpen when a loud crash echoed through the building.

Running into the small gift shop, I found Dad lying on the floor next to a toppled stepladder. He was half-buried beneath a pile of broken plaster and the air was thick with dust. Looking up, I saw a section of the ceiling had collapsed, leaving wooden slats hanging down like broken ribs.

"Are you all right?" I demanded as I clambered over the debris to reach him. "Don't move. I'll call an ambulance."

"Don't you dare," Dad growled. "I'm fine…"

"Don't move. You may have broken something," I said, but he struggled to his feet. "

"Nonsense. We have to get this mess cleared up."

"But are you sure you're okay? What happened?"

"What does it look like? I was up the ladder painting the ceiling when a bloody great section let go and fell on my head. Luckily, I landed on my backside, so no damage done."

"I still think you should see a doctor."

"Forget the doctor. What I need is a builder," Dad said firmly. "See if you can find Steve."

I knew when to give up.

I left Dad shaking plaster from his hair, and by the time I returned with Steve, he had scraped the debris into a corner and was staring up at the hole above him.

"Morning, Steve," he said. "Any chance you can get that filled in by lunchtime? If so, I'll paint it as soon as it's set."

~

Phil was the only one who was ahead of schedule and the news the Animal Meadow was filled with friendly creatures waiting to welcome our guests gave us all a lift.

Having finished the feeding and cleaning routines for the morning, Phil was working with Bob in the shop.

The bay window in the gift shop had a window seat in it, which was big enough to hold the entire family. It had become a favourite spot for tea breaks and Abbie helped me carry in a tray halfway through the morning.

I was delighted by the way the shop was coming together. The new display units were far more spacious and well-designed than the ones we had used in the Barn.

We had tried to include something for every taste and the stock ranged from Devon recipe cookbooks and handmade hats to souvenir bookmarks and pocket money toys.

We had brought the brassware and jewellery that had proved so popular in the Spanish Barn but now everything was beautifully displayed on purpose-built stands with overhead lighting picking out the most impressive pieces. I was certain our visitors would love it.

As I poured the tea, I sensed something was wrong. Bob seemed more tense than usual.

"Is everything okay?" I asked him.

"Everything except that idiot, Paddy. I was arranging the necklaces on the stand earlier when I had to go up to the office to make some phone calls. Phil had gone to the storeroom, but when I came back, Paddy was in here and the stand and the necklaces were scattered all over the floor. I asked him what had happened, and he made a whole deal about it being Fred, whoever Fred is."

"That's the name they use for the ghost."

"Really? If you ask me, this whole ghost thing is getting out of hand. Someone's playing stupid tricks and it's not funny."

~

On the way back to the Devon Mysteries, I found Tom the Potter balancing precariously on a ladder halfway up the back staircase. He was painting the window frames and leaving large white splashes over the glass as he went.

"Shouldn't you have masking tape on the windows?" I asked, but he shook his head impatiently.

"Takes too much time. Much faster to scrape the excess off with a blade once it's dry."

I was too tired to argue with him.

As he leaned sideways, the ladder wobbled alarmingly.

"Is that safe?" I asked.

"Of course it is," Tom replied. "I have an excellent sense of balance."

"Good," I muttered, "because I don't have time to take you to hospital."

~

The rest of the day was a stream of minor problems and irritations. No single issue was critical, but together, they took up a lot of valuable time and energy. By the end of the day, there was hardly anything I could cross off my to-do list.

Once the workers had left, Bob and I stood in the kitchen and listened to the silence. Claire played quietly in her playpen, and for once, the old house seemed at peace.

"Come here." Bob held out an arm to me, and as I leaned against him, a wave of exhaustion swept over me. I could have slept for a month.

"What do you want to eat?" he asked.

"Nothing."

"You have to eat something. You didn't stop for lunch."

"Abbie made me a big breakfast," I said, without mentioning I had never found time to eat it.

"I'll make an omelette. That's quick and easy."

"I'm really not hungry."

"Don't argue."

"Mamma!" Claire pulled herself upright and held her hands out to me.

"Why don't you take her for a walk while I cook?" Bob suggested. "It won't be long."

Claire burbled happily as we wandered along the corridor, pointing to each door and window as we passed, chattering to herself in words I couldn't understand.

As we approached the gift shop, someone was whistling, and she stopped and looked up at me.

"Who's that?" I asked.

"Ganddad!" Claire giggled. "Ganddad, Ganddad!"

She tottered to the door of the small gift shop, then looked back at me with a puzzled expression.

Steve must have re-plastered the ceiling because Dad was balanced on a stepladder, rollering white paint across the ceiling. Unfortunately, because the new plaster was still so wet, drips of water and paint were falling like rain.

"Is that paint going to stay up there?" I asked.

"Maybe it will and maybe it won't," Dad said without slowing down, "but they're laying the carpet in here tomorrow, so it's worth a try."

His hair, face and clothes were splattered white, and for the first time in days, I found myself laughing.

"I can get you an umbrella, if you like," I offered.

When the carpet layers returned in the morning, the ceiling in the small gift shop was still dripping. Timothy looked at the white puddles splattered across the floor and shook his head in disbelief.

"I'm sure it will stop soon," I said hopefully. "Perhaps you'd better leave this room until last."

I found David and told him we had a problem.

"There has to be something we can do. What about a dehumidifier?"

"It might help," he agreed. "I'll see what I can arrange."

The doorbell rang, and I was startled to find Mr Turner standing outside. On a normal day, I would have been happy to see him, but this was anything but a normal day, and I had a sudden, irrational fear that if I let him into the house, he might spot some last-minute problem.

"I was passing, so I thought I'd call in and say hello. Is everything ready?"

I did my best to look calm and collected.

"Oh, yes, we're practically finished."

He grinned as Paddy dragged a wheelbarrow of broken plaster out of the gift shop behind me.

"I can see that."

"Don't worry. Last minute tidying up, that's all. Actually, while you're here, there's something I want to ask you."

I stepped past him and was relieved when he followed me to the bank of wild flowers.

"Do you know anything about these? The purple flowers with the patterns all over them. I've never seen anything like them before."

"They're beautiful, aren't they?" Mr Turner smiled. "Those are fritillaries. Snake's head fritillaries, to be exact. As it happens, I've been meaning to talk to you about them."

"Really? Why?"

"Because they're protected. You do know the grounds

here are listed as an area of outstanding floral interest, don't you?"

"No. Is that a problem?"

"Not at all. But it does mean you can only cut the grass twice a year."

My heart raced immediately.

"But how are we supposed to keep the lawn under control if we can't cut it?"

He smiled at my shocked expression. "Don't worry, it doesn't apply to the lawns. Only the banks and the areas under the trees."

I let out a sigh of relief.

"But it does mean you can't disturb the plants. You can't dig them up to make flowerbeds or anything like that."

"Don't worry, we don't intend to disturb anything," I assured him. "We love the wildflowers."

"I'm glad to hear it. They are spectacular, aren't they? But it might be a good idea to put up a notice somewhere to let the public know the flowers are protected. Technically, it's a criminal offence to pick one. We wouldn't want anyone getting arrested, would we?"

Much as I liked Mr Turner, I didn't have any time to spare, so when I saw Tom the Potter walking along the drive I waved at him.

"Morning, Tom. Would you mind showing Mr Turner how great the craft units look now?"

"It would be a pleasure," Tom said breezily, "and don't worry about the window on the back staircase. I finished painting it yesterday."

~

"Where's Paddy?"

Bob's outburst made me jump.

"Why? What's happened?"

"I've had enough of his stupid tricks! Where is he?"

"Slow down. What are you talking about? "

Bob took a deep breath and I could see he was struggling to keep his temper.

"I was in the shop, putting up a row of cup hooks to hang the horse brasses, but there were two hooks short. I knew I'd had the right number because I'd counted them out and Paddy was the only other person there, so it must have been him that took them."

"Did you ask him?"

"No. I was as irritated as hell, but I knew he was only doing it to annoy me, so I decided not to react. I went back to the storeroom to get two more."

He hesitated and took another deep breath.

"And...?"

"When I got back, the whole row of cup hooks had been unscrewed and laid in a row on the floor. I don't have time to waste on this stupidity."

Bob's eyes were dark with shadows, and I knew he was as tired as I was.

"I'm sorry," I said quietly, "but I don't think it was Paddy. He was complaining yesterday that his nails had disappeared."

"Well, if it's not him, it must be one of the other builders. We're not paying them to waste our time with stupid pranks."

"I know it's annoying, but this isn't the time for a showdown," I pleaded. "We only have one more day. Can't you just ignore it for a little bit longer?"

He exhaled and clenched his fists. "I suppose so, but it's so bloody childish."

"I know it is, but if the builders walk out now, we'll be stuffed."

"All right," Bob agreed reluctantly, "but keep them away from me. And I don't want to hear one more thing about this bloody ghost!"

The rest of the day was spent dealing with one crisis after another. The power supply to the freezers cut out just as our first delivery of frozen catering supplies arrived. Trevor, our electrician, saved the day by installing a new cable but he had barely put his tools away before Phil rushed in to tell us one of the goats had escaped from the Animal Meadow, and chewed through a pile of gift boxes in the glass engravers' unit.

In the afternoon, a cistern in the ladies' toilets sprang a leak, flooding half the corridor, and the newly installed fire alarm system kept going off for no obvious reason.

By the end of the day, tempers were frayed.

"I thought the floors were supposed to be finished today?" David demanded when he spotted the carpet layer's van driving out of the gate.

"That was the plan," I agreed, "but we've still got tomorrow. It's still possible."

David wasn't convinced.

"Don't tell me that," he grumbled. "Nothing's gone smoothly today. If it's the same tomorrow, we haven't got a hope of being ready."

"Can't you be a bit more positive?" I snapped. "There's no point in looking for problems."

"I don't have to look for them!" David snapped back. "Everything's gone wrong. There are still two whole exhibitions to wire up. We might as well face it now. We haven't got a hope."

"Yes, we have," I said obstinately. "We still have one more day."

The stress must have affected Claire because she decided not to sleep that night either. Bob and I took it in turns to walk around the bedroom in a zombie-like state while she grizzled and pulled at our hair.

Finally, I gave up.

"I'm not wasting any more time," I said. "If she doesn't want to sleep, she will have to stay with me."

I strapped Claire into her buggy and headed back to the Enchanted Forest. She watched with wide eyes as I pulled out my paints and brushes. It was the quietest she had been for hours.

At first, Claire was content to watch as I swished the brush across the wall, leaving green leaf shapes behind it. I had put on some soothing music and hoped she would get bored and fall asleep, but I had underestimated my daughter's artistic interests.

"Mumma!" she burbled happily, holding out a chubby hand towards the paint tins. "Me, me!"

"No, Claire, this is for Mummy, not you."

"Me, me, me!"

"Please, darling, Mummy has to work."

"Me, me, me!"

"We can draw with your crayons another day. Please be good for Mummy now."

"Me, me, me!"

"No, Claire. Play with your teddy."

"Waah!"

I dropped the brush and pushed the buggy around the room.

"Please... Go to sleep," I begged. I loved Claire dearly, but I was exhausted.

"I can't do this anymore," I sobbed as I walked. "I just can't do it."

"Here, let me have a go."

Bob stood behind me, his eyes half-closed. "She'll settle faster for me."

It was true. Claire loved her Daddy and snuggled her face into his neck the moment he picked her up. I felt like a failure. I should have been able to do it all.

I didn't have time to read women's magazines unless I was at the dentist's but I had glanced through enough articles to know that successful women were expected to hold down high-powered jobs, raise perfectly behaved children, and still look as though they had just walked out of a Vogue photoshoot. It was 1986 and modern wives weren't supposed to need any help from their husbands.

I didn't care. At that moment, it didn't matter if I was a rubbish wife and a hopeless mother. All that mattered was that I needed to rest.

I lay on the floor, put my head on an old towel, and was asleep in seconds.

I was woken by the squeak of the buggy's wheels as Bob pushed it along the corridor.

Guiltily, I sat up, grabbed a brush, and pretended I had been hard at work.

"She's asleep," Bob whispered as he rolled the buggy to a stop beside me. "Are you okay?"

"I'm fine."

"Remember, get past Saturday and you can have an early night. Are you stopping yet?"

"Soon. You go up to bed. I just need to finish this wall and I'll be up."

"Do you want me to take Claire?"

"No, I'll bring her up with me in a minute."

"Okay," he yawned, "Don't be long."

I knew that if I didn't finish the mural then, I wouldn't have another chance and I couldn't bear the thought of children coming into the Enchanted Forest and finding half-painted tree trunks on the walls.

My short nap had made a difference. I no longer felt defeated. Picking up my brushes, I started again.

I was still painting at seven-thirty. Early morning sunlight gleamed outside when David appeared beside me.

"You'd better come. We've got a problem."

I followed him to the tearooms, pushing the buggy ahead of me, and gasped.

Dad, Steve and Paddy were gathered around a huge hole in the floor. Splintered floorboards disappeared into the darkness below, and dust and dirt hung in the air.

"What happened?" I asked.

"It was Paddy," David said unnecessarily.

"Sure, it wasn't my fault," Paddy protested. "I was doing nothing but stand there, and the next moment, I was up to my knees in splinters, so I was."

"What are we going to do?" I demanded. "The carpet layers will be here any minute."

"They're here already," Paddy corrected me. "They're getting their gear out the van right now."

Steve knelt beside the hole, prodding the exposed joists with a screwdriver.

"There are no signs of rot. That's something. It looks like it's just one joist that's given way."

"Here, let me see." Dad dropped to his knees beside Steve and peered into the dusty space.

"Look, the joist had a knot in it and the wood's splintered from there."

"Having a few tons of rock piled on it wouldn't have helped," David muttered, glancing at Paddy.

"But what are we going to do?" I repeated. "How long will it take to fix it?"

Steve scratched his chin.

"We'll have to take the boards up to get at it. That's going to be difficult as the counter's built over them. Whichever way you look at it, it's going to take a while."

"But we don't have time!"

"Is there any of that steel plate left?" Dad asked suddenly.

David shrugged.

"I'm not sure, but if there is, it will be up in your storeroom."

Dad scrambled to his feet.

"Don't do anything until we get back."

A few minutes later, he and David returned carrying an enormous sheet of steel plate.

"We can use this," Dad said.

There was a cloud of dust as they lowered the steel to the floor.

"But what are you going to do with it?" I asked.

"I've done it," Dad said simply. "It'll spread the weight across the whole floor for the time being. No one's going to fall through that. We can carpet over it."

"You can't do that!" I protested. "Mr Turner wouldn't approve."

"No. I'm sure he wouldn't," Dad agreed. "But he's not here, is he? And it's going to be covered in carpet any minute, so he's never going to see it."

"But is it safe?"

"I wouldn't do it if it wasn't safe. Here, I'll dance on it for you if you like."

"Don't worry," Steve agreed, "he's right. You could drive a car over that. It's perfectly safe."

"And it's only for the summer," Dad promised. "Once the season's over, we'll take the carpet up and repair it all properly."

"I really don't think we should…" I began, but Dad held up his hand.

"Objection noted, but you're outvoted. Go and tell the carpet layers they can get started."

The carpet layers were working on the back staircase when I found them.

Looking up, I was horrified to see the windows above them were blotched with thick daubs of white paint.

Hurrying across to the craft block, I found Tom singing happily to himself as he laid out pots on a circular display table.

"Tom, you've forgotten the windows," I blurted out. "They're still covered in paint."

"I know," he said. "I told you they would need to be scraped off with a blade."

"I thought you meant you were going to do it."

"Me? Certainly not. I'm a painter, not a scraper. In any case, I can't help you anymore. I have to get my displays ready. You do realise we are opening tomorrow, don't you?"

Finally, my patience ran out.

"I shouldn't have shouted at him," I admitted to Bob later, "but I just couldn't stop myself."

"Don't keep thinking about it. The windows will have to stay as they are for now. The good news is the carpet layers say they will be able to finish everything today."

"They think? They're not leaving until it's done. If they even try, I'll get one of Farmer Alan's cattle prods and block the exit."

I was only half joking.

The carpet layers worked until late in the evening, but by the time they left, all the rooms, halls and stairs of Silverlands were covered in pristine new carpet.

It was a huge relief, but there was still plenty to do.

Martha and Abbie had volunteered to work late and by the time they left, the furniture in the tearooms was in place on the new carpet and each table displayed a pretty tablecloth and place settings.

In the kitchen, the sinks and counters gleamed, and everything was ready for action.

But we were still not finished. I left Bob and Phil pricing the last items in the shop and headed up to the Devon Mysteries. I needed to complete the final background scene for the Beast of Dartmoor display.

The legendary Beast is a massive, leopard-like cat that roams the moors and the display featured a black cat's head, about the size of a lion, with its lips drawn back in a snarl, revealing an enormous set of white fangs.

We kept the window of the Beast's display small so people would be tempted to step up to see what was inside. Once they got close enough, a detector triggered a flash of lightning that illuminated the Beast's head immediately in front of them.

All I had left to do was to paint a lifelike moorland scene behind the Beast and I could go to bed, but before I could start, I heard footsteps hurrying towards me.

"I'm sorry, but there's a problem..."

David sounded desperate.

"I don't understand it. There's something wrong with the wiring in the First World War exhibition, but I can't find what it is. I've been through everything three times, but I can't run the controls and see what's happening at the same time."

"Do you want me to come and help you?" I offered.

"I'm really sorry. I don't want to stop you, but I'm never going to get it sorted on my own."

"It's OK. I'll wipe out my brushes and be with you."

An hour later, when Bob came searching for me, David and I were pulling the wiring from the back of a display.

"It doesn't make any sense," David complained. "There's nothing wrong when I test the sections individually, but the moment they are all connected, it stops working. There has to be a glitch somewhere, but I can't find it."

"We've decided it will be faster to rewire the display rather than waste any more time trying to find the problem." I sighed.

"Can I help?" Bob offered, but I shook my head.

"Mum's still looking after Claire," I reminded him. "We can't keep her up any longer. You'd better put Claire to bed and get some sleep yourself. One of us has to be awake enough to welcome everyone tomorrow."

"Are you sure?"

"Of course. I'm going to be in the kitchen anyway, so no one will notice if I'm dead on my feet."

Reluctantly, Bob went up while I cut lengths of wire for David.

It was past five o'clock in the morning before we finished.

"Is it worth going to bed?" David asked as we packed the tools away.

"You might as well grab an hour's sleep if you can."

"What about you?"

"I've still got to finish the Beast of Dartmoor, but it shouldn't take long."

"Is there anything I can do to help?"

"No. Get some rest while you can. It's going to be a busy day."

I painted quickly, slapping dark colours across the wall in what I hoped was a passable impression of the moors at night, but as I worked, my eyelids drooped. I tried stretching, biting my lips, singing loudly to myself, but nothing helped. I even took off my shoes and socks, so the cold floor chilled my feet, but my mind still teetered on the edge of sleep.

Finally, I stepped back and looked at what I had done.

It was truly awful.

For a moment, I wanted to cry. There was no time left. I had failed.

In a fit of depression, I reached inside the display and unscrewed the light bulb. When people complained the display was not working, I would claim it was an electrical fault.

With a heavy heart, I gathered my paints and brushes and headed downstairs.

The sun was up and birds sang outside. It was too late to sleep, so I went for a quick shower instead.

CHAPTER 15

Bob and Claire

As I came downstairs, music drifted from the shop and long shafts of sunlight sparkled across the cutlery on the tearoom tables.

Claire waved a piece of toast at me from her highchair.

"Look, it's Mummy," Bob said with a smile. "You've forgotten what she looks like, haven't you?"

"Don't be mean," I protested, but Claire giggled and held out her arms to me.

"You realise you haven't been to bed for three nights now?"

"Are you sure?" I groaned. "It feels more like three weeks."

"Why don't you put your head down for a bit?" he suggested. "No one's going to arrive before ten."

"If I close my eyes now, I won't wake up for a week. Don't worry, I'm fine."

"Then have some breakfast. What do you want? Cereal? Bacon? Porridge?"

"Nothing. I'm not hungry."

Bob gave me a disapproving look.

"When did you last eat anything?"

"I don't remember, please don't start..."

"Then don't argue. I'm going to get you some breakfast and you're going to eat it. Okay?"

I didn't answer, but I felt the familiar knot tightening in my stomach. I didn't want to eat.

A moment later, Bob plopped a plate on the table in front of me. Two enormous slices of sticky, chocolate-covered flapjack buried beneath a mound of clotted cream.

A delicious aroma wafted up from them, and to my surprise, I found my mouth watering.

"They're still warm," Bob said. "The baker's just delivered them."

"You are an angel," I breathed and reached for a fork.

~

We had printed 10 am on the official invitations, and by nine-thirty, we were all gathered in the tearooms, ready to take up our positions. The air was alive with expectation and unasked questions. No one put their thoughts into words, but we all shared the same doubts.

Dad coughed loudly, and everyone turned to him.

"I just want to say that, however things go today, I couldn't be more proud of you all. What we've done here in the last few months, well, it's been a bit of a miracle really, hasn't it?"

"It's a miracle we're still sane, if that's what you mean," David grinned.

"And it's a miracle no one's killed Paddy," Bob added.

Our laughter was interrupted by Abbie bursting in from the corridor.

"Quick," she gasped, "there's a rat in the disabled loo."

"No!" I cried. "I thought they'd all gone."

"I'm sorry. Let's hope it's the last one."

I left David to deal with the rat and helped Mum carry her bag of tickets, souvenir programmes and spare change down to the ticket box. By the time she had sorted herself out, it was five minutes to ten.

I squeezed in beside her and perched and she took my hand and squeezed my fingers.

"Here we go."

We waited in silence as the minutes ticked by.

"What do we do if no one comes?" I asked.

Mum looked out across the lawns for a long moment before she answered.

"We'll have to eat a lot of cream teas."

Outside, birds hopped on the lawn and bees buzzed around the blossom of an old Judas tree. Then there was the sound of a car grinding its gears as it climbed the hill to the car park. It was followed by another, and a few minutes later, two figures appeared outside the ticket box.

I was not surprised to see our first guest was Mr Turner, but I was astounded that he was accompanied by Mr Wooley, our old bank manager. The two of them were chatting like long-lost friends.

"Hello," I greeted them. "I'm delighted you could make it."

"I wouldn't have missed it for the world," Mr Wooley assured me. "It's not every day one of my customers proves me wrong."

"She doesn't give in easily. I'll give her that," Mr Turner smiled.

"Told me to my face, she did," Mr Wooley continued. "I'm going to prove you wrong, and I'll send you an invitation to the grand opening. I have to say, I didn't think you'd be able to pull it off, but here I am, ready to be impressed."

I felt like a child being praised by her teachers.

I was pleased they were pleased, but I wanted them to move on and visit the house. I intended to hide in the ticket box for as long as possible.

"Why don't you show our friends what we've done?" Mum suggested. "I can manage here."

I searched for an excuse, but could think of nothing.

On the way up the drive, the two men chatted, and I discovered they had gone to school together.

"John was always the clever one," Mr Turner told me. "I always knew he'd end up running his own bank one day."

"If only!" Mr Wooley laughed. "I'm a very small cog in a vast machine. Bank managers have very little autonomy these days."

As we approached the house, Abbie was on the tea lawn, putting tiny vases of flowers on the tables. I smiled. She really was trying hard. Then I recognised the delicate purple flowers.

"Shall we go in through the main entrance?" I veered to the left, shepherding the men away from the tea lawns. "Please make sure you see everything, but if you'll excuse me, I think I'm needed."

I ran to the tearooms and grabbed Abbie's arm.

"Get the vases off the tables!"

"Why?"

"Just do it!"

I handed her a tray and grabbed another for myself. Between us, we zipped around the tables, collecting the vases.

"I thought you'd be pleased," Abbie said dejectedly as she looked at the jugs of flowers lined up in the kitchen.

"I'm sorry. I didn't mean to shout at you, but these are fritillaries. It's against the law to pick them."

Abbie's eyes opened wide. "I didn't know. Am I going to get in trouble?"

Her face was a picture of misery, so I gave her a quick hug.

"Don't worry. Nobody will ever know."

I spent the rest of the day rushing from place to place, checking everything was running smoothly. Sometimes I was behind the servery counter filling teapots with steaming water, sometimes I was refilling shelves in the gift shop or checking the loo rolls had not run out in the toilets.

I avoided speaking to anyone if I could help it, but I listened avidly and all the conversations seemed positive. Many of our guests had brought their children with them, and they all appeared to be having a good time. The circus was as popular as ever, and the new exhibition rooms were full.

To be on the safe side, I turned the music up everywhere in case there were still any rat noises. I listened all the time, but the house was so full of voices I heard nothing.

The local TV crew turned up and Bob welcomed them, dressed in his ringmaster's outfit. Through the tearoom window, I watched him being interviewed on the lawn before disappearing with the camera crew to film the various exhibitions and the craft block.

When he returned, Bob was elated.

"That was amazing! They had only planned to do a few shots, but they loved everything so much they've made it much longer. They did a lovely interview with your dad about the circus and they're going to make it into a proper feature. It will be fantastic advertising for us."

"That's wonderful!" I beamed. "It's exactly what we need. And everyone else seems happy too, so hopefully word will get around all the coach companies as well."

When the last of our guests left, we gathered in the tearooms and compared notes on how the day had gone.

"I think we should all be pleased with ourselves," David said. "I was talking to one of the photographers and he was confident he'll be able to get articles into all the local papers and even some of the nationals."

"And one of the radio guys wants to come back another weekend and do an outside broadcast," Bob added.

Phil beamed.

"You mean a roadshow? That will be awesome!"

"But right now, we can all have an early night," Mum said.

"I wish I could, but I've still got to finish the background for the Beast of Dartmoor display." I sighed, but David jumped in.

"No, don't change it. It's perfect as it is."

"What do you mean? It's not working. I took the bulb out."

"You might have taken the bulb out, but you forgot about the lightning effect. Because it's so dark, people go right up to the glass to see what's inside and they trigger the motion sensor. It's brilliant. The lightning flashes and the Beast is right there in front of them. It's a real shock and everyone loves it."

"Oh God! I forgot about the lightning effect," I gasped. "I meant to finish it tonight."

"We're not changing it now," David said firmly. "One kid said his mother nearly died of fright and her reaction was the funniest thing he'd ever seen."

"Well, if you're sure."

"Yes, it's decided. The Beast stays as it is and we all get to sleep tonight."

The next day was completely different.

Instead of welcoming invited guests, we opened Silverlands to the public for the first time, and faced a whole new range of problems.

After the excitement of the previous day, I was afraid I would struggle to keep awake, but I need not have worried. There was plenty to keep me busy, and I remember the day as being a whirl of activity and changing faces.

It soon became clear we had underestimated the amount of staff we needed in the kitchen. Once people began ordering lunches, Abbie and I found ourselves running to keep up and we had no time to clear the

A juggler in action.

tables. Dad came in to get a cup of tea for Mum, but when he saw that every table in the tearooms was covered in dirty crockery, he spent the rest of the day clearing them. The dishwasher never stopped and none of us got a break all day.

Outside, the weather was beautiful and I could hear laughter and applause from the crowd watching the live entertainment on the lawn.

. . .

Bob told me he had gone over to the craft block at one point and had been pleased to see demonstrations going on in every unit.

As the afternoon wore on, the crowds thinned and Abbie, Dad and I finally caught up with the dishwasher.

It was a huge relief to know our visitors were enjoying the exhibitions, and I felt sure the summer season was going to be a great success.

There were still a few things that weren't quite finished, but the only thing that really mattered was that the customers were happy.

Tiredness crept up on me again, but I loved every moment. The afternoon light slanted through the bay windows, bathing everything in a warm glow. I had never been so happy in my life.

When the public left, we had the old building to ourselves again and gathered in the tearoom for our daily ritual. As I poured the tea, Bob asked me if there had been any unexplained happenings.

"Nothing that I know about."

"No sign of Fred?"

"Not a thing."

"I was right," he said triumphantly. "The builders have gone and I'll bet we never hear anything again."

Later, once Claire was settled in her cot, I headed down to the kitchen.

I had popped some bread into the toaster and was heating a pan of beans over a gas ring when I felt guilty. Bob had insisted he only wanted something simple, but he deserved more than beans on toast.

Pulling open a cupboard, I searched for anything that

would pass as a treat and was pleased to find a single tin of plums.

I took it out, placed it on the counter, and turned to find a tin opener in the drawer behind me.

As I turned back, the tin was gone.

I stared at the empty counter in disbelief. Where was it? There was nothing else on the counter and the floor below was clear.

Confusion filled my brain. I knew I had placed the tin there, right in front of me, and yet now it had gone.

Stupidly, I opened the cupboard to check I really had taken the tin out. Yes, there was no tin of plums there.

I looked again at the empty counter. Then at the floor. This was not possible.

There was no one else in the kitchen and the door into the corridor was closed. Even if it had been open, I knew no one could have come in and taken the tin in the time it had taken me to turn away and pick up the tin opener.

I ran my fingers over the counter as if expecting to find a hidden trapdoor. Nothing.

There was no explanation. Nothing that made sense. Nothing that could reassure me my world was safe. I was tired and stressed, and now a wave of panic threatened to overwhelm me. Leaning against the counter, I buried my head in my hands.

Behind me, the kitchen door clunked open.

"Are you okay?"

It was Dad's voice.

"No, not really."

"Why? What's up?"

I heard his footsteps come towards me and felt the reassuring weight of his hand on my shoulder.

"What's up?" he asked again.

As I straightened, I realised my face was wet with tears.

Pulling a tissue from his pocket, Dad unfolded it and held it out to me.

I wiped my eyes and blew my nose.

"There really is a ghost," I said.

"Have you seen it?"

"No, but either there's a ghost or I'm as crazy as Granny."

"You're not crazy. Listen, love, I don't know anything about ghosts, but I do know there are things in this world we don't understand. This is an old house and if there is a ghost here, so what?"

"But things keep happening!"

"You mean the footsteps and the lights?"

"It's more than that. It stole my plums."

Dad's expression had been serious, but now his face creased into a grin.

"What in hell would a ghost want with your plums?"

"How should I know?" I sniffed. "But they've gone. A whole tin. Just like that."

"So, you're telling me there's a ghost-fella floating around in here, looking down on us while he's slurping your plums?"

The Australian twang in Dad's voice was always strongest when he was amused, and I smiled despite myself.

"It's not funny!" I protested. "I'm serious. There really is a ghost. Or a spirit, or something… I thought it was someone playing jokes, but this time it couldn't have been a trick. The tin vanished. One moment, it was there. The next, it was gone."

"In that case, I guess there's only one answer."

"What's that?"

"You'll have to have rice pudding."

"You're not taking this seriously!" I pouted.

"I am taking it seriously, but let's say you're right. Suppose there is a ghost. What do you think we should do about it?"

"That's the point. I have no idea what to do."

"Well, maybe we should think about things from Fred's perspective. He was probably very happy here with the whole place to himself. Then, one day, we arrive and turn everything upside down without even asking him. Perhaps he's entitled to a few tricks."

"I hadn't thought of it like that."

"Trust me, love, I've been through plenty of difficult times in my life. I've been stabbed in the back by people I trusted and let down by others that I thought were my friends, but never, not once, have I been hurt by a ghost."

He handed me another tissue.

"If you want my advice, it's simple. Don't waste your time worrying about dead people, it's the live buggers you have to watch out for."

He was right. If I could cope with temperamental craftspeople, obstinate planning officers, manic neighbours and an infestation of rats, surely I could cope with one unpredictable ghost?

"Thanks, I guess you're right."

"I'm always right. You know that."

I wiped my eyes and hugged him. There was a wonderful simplicity about Dad. He always knew how to keep things in perspective.

What really mattered was that we had achieved our goal. We had worked together as a team and overcome all the obstacles that had been thrown at us. Surely nothing could stop us now?

At that moment, I felt I could face anything.

Of course, I might have felt differently if I had known what lay ahead.

ABOUT THE AUTHOR

Writing has always been a part of my life as my mother wrote books, magazine stories and even TV plays, in the days when dramas were transmitted live.

Over the years, I have written plays for schools and community groups as well as scripts, two of which have been produced as feature films.

I began writing books during the pandemic and loved the experience so much I decided to keep going. My first complete series was a set of memoirs under the title Me, My Family and the Poltergeist which explains how my family and I came to share a derelict school with an uninvited guest.

Most recently, I have partnered with my brother, David Hardie, to write and illustrate a series of children's books about the Dittos of Dawlish, a magical race of elf-like creature who look after wildlife and recycle items humans leave behind.

I am lucky enough to live near the sea in Devon, England with my husband, Robert. I love walking on the beach and I even swim occasionally, but only in the summer when it's VERY hot.

Printed in Dunstable, United Kingdom

72491626R00163